Brendan Scott is the author and editor of numerous books and articles relating to religion and society in early modern Ireland, with a particular focus on Cavan. He is the manager of the Irish Family History Foundation and is the editor of the *Breifne* history journal.

# A RELATION

OF

The beginnings and proceedings of the Rebellion in the County of *Cavan*, within the Province of ULSTER in IRELAND, From the 23. of *October*, 1641. untill the 15. of *June*, 1642. Whereof hitherto nothing hath been reported.

Whereunto is added, The Acts, and twenty nine Conclusions of that great and generall Congregation

OF

Archbishops, Bishops, and others, All of the Romish Clergy in IRELAND, met in the City of *Kilkenny* in that Kingdom, on the 10 11 and 13 of *May*, 1642.

Concerning the present State of the Warre in IRELAND; and for the ordering of matters appertaining to the same, both there, and by Negotiation with forraign Princes.

Written, set forth, and presented to the most Honourable the Houses of Parliament, By *Henry Iones*, D. D.

There is also added a Letter written from *Dublin*, *August* 4. 1642. Containing some late and very remarkable passages in IRELAND.

---

*August* 11. *London*, Printed for *Godfrey Emerson*, and are to be sold at the signe of the Swan in Little-*Britain*, 1642.

Henry Jones, *A relation of the beginnings and proceedings of the rebellion in the county of Cavan, within the province of Ulster in Ireland, from the 23 of October, 1641, untill the 15 of June, 1642* (London, 1642)

# Dr Henry Jones' Account of the 1641 Rising

PLANTATION AND WAR
IN COUNTY CAVAN

*Edited by*
Brendan Scott

ULSTER HISTORICAL FOUNDATION

Old cathedral and bishop's palace, Kilmore.
Courtesy of the National Library of Ireland

*For Raymond Gillespie,*
*in recognition of his scholarship and generosity*

The author and Ulster Historical Foundation are pleased to acknowledge support for this publication from Cavan County Heritage Office and the Church of Ireland General Synod Royalties Fund.

COVER IMAGES

Henry Jones, artist unattributed, oil on canvas: collection of Trinity College, Dublin. Image courtesy of and reproduced by permission of the Board of Trinity College, Dublin, the University of Dublin; Deposition of Henry Jones: TCD, MS 840, fo. 32v. © The Board of Trinity College, Dublin; engraving from James Cranford, the *Teares of Ireland*, 1642

INSIDE FRONT COVER

Excerpt from *Partie septentr, le du royume d'Irlande, ou sont la province d'Ulster, et partie des prov.ces* [sic] *de Leinster, et Connaugh* (1665). Library of Congress, Geography and Map Division

Published 2021
by Ulster Historical Foundation
www.ancestryireland.com
www.booksireland.org.uk

Except as otherwise permitted under the Copyright, Designs and Patents Act 1988, this publication may only be reproduced, stored or transmitted in any form or by any means with the prior permission in writing of the publisher or, in the case of reprographic reproduction, in accordance with the terms of a licence issued by The Copyright Licensing Agency. Enquiries concerning reproduction outside those terms should be sent to the publisher.

© Brendan Scott and Ulster Historical Foundation
ISBN 978-1-913993-09-2

DESIGN AND FORMATTING
FPM Publishing

COVER DESIGN AND PLATE SECTION
J.P. Morrison

PRINTED BY
Bell & Bain Limited

# Contents

| | |
|---|---|
| LIST OF FIGURES IN THE PLATE SECTION | viii |
| PREFACE AND ACKNOWLEDGEMENTS | ix |
| ABBREVIATIONS | xi |
| NOTE ON THE TEXT | xi |

| | |
|---|---|
| Introduction: Henry Jones and Cavan, 1610–42 | 1 |
| Henry Jones' *Relation* | 33 |

APPENDICES

| | |
|---|---|
| 1  The acts of the synod of Kilkenny, May 1642 | 64 |
| 2  Letter: Hugh Culme to Henry Jones, 4 August 1642 | 71 |
| 3  Remonstrance from County of Cavan to Lords Justices and Council at Dublin, 6th November 1641 and the response of the Council | 73 |
| BIBLIOGRAPHY | 76 |
| INDEX | 81 |

# List of Figures in the Plate Section

Figure 1: Henry Jones, artist unattributed, oil on canvas: collection of Trinity College, Dublin. Image courtesy of and reproduced by permission of the Board of Trinity College, Dublin, the University of Dublin

Figure 2: William Bedell's tombstone, Kilmore cathedral churchyard. Courtesy of William Roulston

Figure 3: Old cathedral and bishop's palace, Kilmore. Courtesy of William Roulston

Figure 4: Deposition of Henry Jones: TCD, MS 840, fo. 32v. © The Board of Trinity College, Dublin

Figure 5: Barony of Loughtee, 1609: TNA, MPF 1/52. Courtesy of The National Archives

Figure 6: Barony of Tullyhunco, 1609: TNA, MPF 1/57. Courtesy of The National Archives

Figure 7: Map of Cavan town, *c.* 1590s: TNA, MPF 1/81. Courtesy of The National Archives

Figure 8: Clogh Oughter castle. Courtesy of Conleth Manning

# Preface and Acknowledgements

This book is a newly-edited and annotated edition of a pamphlet published in London in 1642. Written by Henry Jones, the Church of Ireland dean of Kilmore, *A relation of the beginnings and proceedings of the rebellion in the county of Cavan* dealt with the 1641 rising and the events connected to it in County Cavan, where Jones lived at the time of the outbreak of the rebellion. Some of this he was able to relate through first-hand experience. But other sections were recounted to him by settlers from Cavan, stories which he heard either in a personal capacity, or through the witness statements given to the Commission for the Despoiled Subject, which Jones established and chaired. These statements are known to us now as the 1641 depositions and are the most important primary source to survive for seventeenth-century Ireland. This edition can be seen as a complementary source from this period, which not only reinforces information supplied in the depositions themselves, but also provides some new detail not found elsewhere. The pamphlet also stands as a justification for Jones' actions during the initial months of the rising and as such, it makes an important contribution to the historiography of the period.

Professor John Morrill first introduced me over a decade ago to Henry Jones' *Relation*. Since then, I have had cause to refer to this pamphlet on numerous occasions and I wish to thank Professor Morrill for first putting it my way. I also came to know Conleth Manning during his work on Clogh Oughter castle in Cavan, and it was he who first suggested to me that a new edition of the *Relation* would be worth considering. This coincided roughly with the appearance of the 1641 depositions online and it struck me that a new edition of Jones' description of the progress of the 1641 rising in Cavan might indeed be a useful addendum to that magnificent project. I also thank Con for supplying the image of Clogh Oughter.

Ulster Historical Foundation, the publishers of this book, have been very supportive over the years, in particular Fintan Mullan and Dr William Roulston. William read the entire work prior to publication and I thank him for his friendship, advice and support. Thanks also to Professor Christopher Maginn, who read and commented upon the introduction to the text. My debt to Professor Raymond Gillespie should be obvious from the dedication. Any remaining mistakes must remain mine alone.

My thanks also go to Professor Micheál Ó Siochrú, Dr Annaleigh Margey, Laura Shanahan, Estelle Gittins, Aisling Lockhart, Catherine Giltrap and the Board of Trinity College, Dublin for their assistance with sourcing and reproducing images used in this book. Sarah Gearty drew the map of Cavan's Plantation towns, for which I am extremely appreciative. For various nuggets of information picked up along the way, I wish to thank Monsignor Liam Kelly, Concepta McGovern (Cavan Genealogy), Dr Pádraig Lenihan and Tomás Ó Raghallaigh. The support of the staff of Cavan Library Service, particularly Jonathan Smyth, former County Librarian Tom Sullivan and current County Librarian Emma Clancy, has been invaluable to me in my research, for which I am especially grateful. I am extremely thankful to Anne Marie Curley of the Cavan County Heritage Office, and to the Church of Ireland General Synod Royalties Fund, whose generous subventions made possible the publication of this book.

But as always, it is to my friends and family that my thanks are most due – my parents John and Rose, my sister Sinéad, brother Martin and their families. The events of 2020 and 2021, have, if nothing else, taught me the importance of family and friends and demonstrated what is truly important in life. Paul McCann and Mark McCann in particular were always only a phone call or Whatsapp message away during the various lockdowns, providing much-needed distractions and laughs. But it is to my immediate family that I am most indebted – my wife Tara and my daughters Eva and Muireann, who give me so much. The debt which I owe them all can never be repaid.

# Abbreviations

| | |
|---:|:---|
| *Cal. pat. rolls Ire.* | *Calendar of the patent and close rolls of chancery in Ireland, Henry VIII–James I* |
| *Cal. S.P. Ire.* | *Calendar of the state papers relating to Ireland*, 24 vols (London, 1860–1911) |
| NAI | National Archives of Ireland |
| RIA | Royal Irish Academy |
| *R.S.A.I. Jn.* | *Journal of the Royal Society of Antiquaries of Ireland* |
| TCD | Trinity College, Dublin |
| TNA | The National Archives, London |
| *DIB* | *Dictionary of Irish Biography*, 11 vols (Cambridge, 2009–18) |
| *Oxford DNB* | *Oxford Dictionary of National Biography*, 60 vols (Oxford, 2004) |

# Note on the Text

Some punctuation has been added or altered to aid the reader's comprehension. Grammar and spelling have been modernised, except for place-names and personal names.

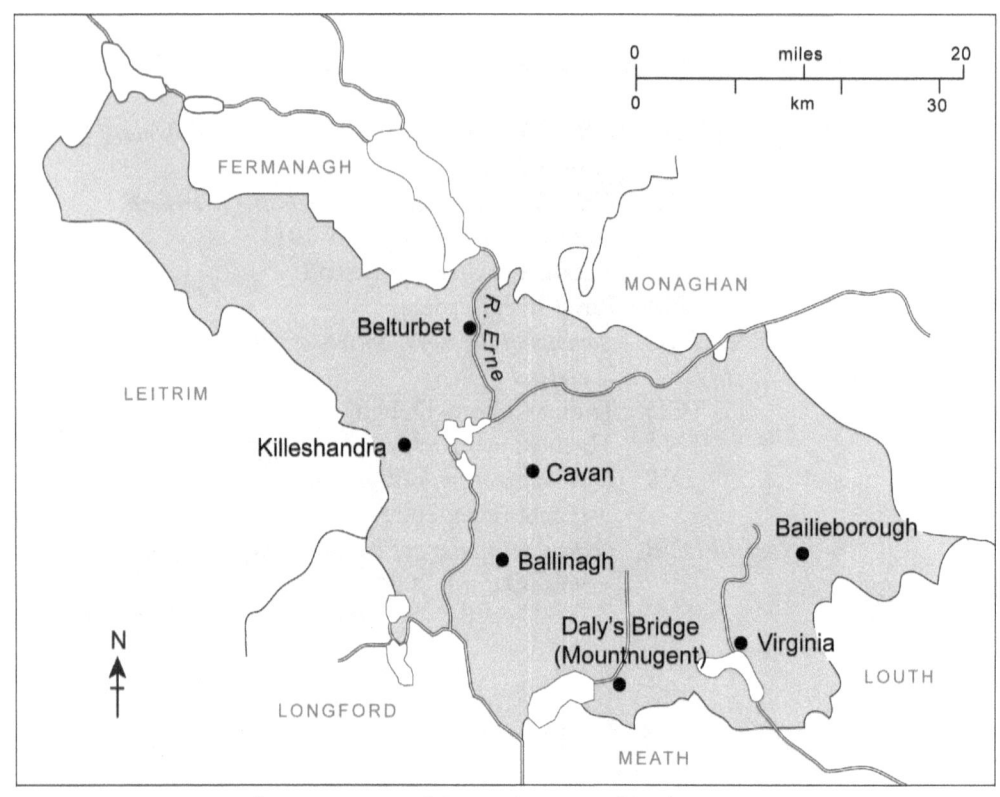

Plantation towns of Cavan. Courtesy of Sarah Gearty

# Introduction
# Henry Jones and Cavan, 1610–42

On 11 August 1642, Dr Henry Jones, the Church of Ireland dean of Kilmore, wrote a short pamphlet which was published in London by Godfrey Emerson. Entitled *A relation of the beginnings and proceedings of the rebellion in the county of Cavan, within the province of Ulster in Ireland, from the 23 of October, 1641, untill the 15 of June, 1642*, the pamphlet, as the title indicates,[1] charted the course of the 1641 rising in County Cavan from its beginnings until the early summer of the following year. Jones established and chaired the 'Commission for the Despoiled Subject', which took the witness statements, mostly from British settlers, now known to us as the 1641 depositions. As such, he had intimate knowledge of the rising and its course to that point, as he not only heard the witness statements, but had also been caught up in the rising himself. The pamphlet he published in August 1642 and which is republished here, is an extremely important document, yet one which has been overlooked to a large degree, overshadowed both by the depositions themselves and Jones' other, more notorious pamphlet, *A remonstrance of divers remarkeable passages concerning the church and kingdom of Ireland*, also published in 1642. Jones' *Relation* (as it shall be referred to throughout this booklet) detailed not only his own experiences, but also those of other British settlers in Cavan during the first months of the rising, when they were faced with robbery, expulsion

---

[1] The full title on the cover page is as follows: *A relation of the beginnings and proceedings of the rebellion in the county of Cavan, within the province of Ulster in Ireland, from the 23 of October, 1641, untill the 15 of June, 1642. Whereof hitherto nothing hath been reported. Whereunto is added, the acts, and twenty nine conclusions of that great and generall congregation of archbishops, bishops, and others, all of the Romish clergy in Ireland, met in the city of Kilkenny in that Kingdom, on the 10, 11 and 13 of May 1642. Concerning the present state of the warre in Ireland, and for the ordering of matters appertaining to the same, both there, and by negotiation with forraign princes. Written, set forth, and presented to the most honourable the Houses of Parliament, By Henry Jones, DD. There is also a letter written from Dublin, August 4 1642. Containing some late and very remarkable passages in Ireland.*

from their homes, violence and sometimes death, either at the hands of the insurgents or indirectly from exposure to the elements in what was a harsh winter that year.

But had Jones paused at the beginning of October 1641 to take stock of the trajectory of his life thus far, he would likely have had cause to feel somewhat pleased with how it had unfolded. Jones, a wealthy man,[2] was married to the daughter of an English planter family in Cavan and had seven children.[3] He had been born into privilege – the eldest son of Lewis Jones, a Welshman who steadily rose up the ranks of the Church of Ireland to become bishop of Killaloe in 1633, and Mabel Ussher. Lewis was from Dollymoch in Wales, and had been a Fellow of All Souls in Oxford in 1568 before moving to Ireland. Lewis Jones first appears in Ireland in 1602, before acquiring numerous positions in the Church of Ireland, including the deanery of Ardagh, which he was granted in 1606, and which he held until 1625. It was in *c.* 1608 that Lewis married Mabel Ussher, who was then aged around twenty at the time of their marriage. Indeed, the significant age gap between them led the antiquarian James Ware to dub Jones the 'vivacious bishop'.[4] Mabel was the daughter of a prominent Dublin family, her parents being Arland Ussher and Margaret Stanihurst, whose grandfather James had been speaker in the Irish parliament. Among Mabel's brothers was James Ussher, one of the seventeenth-century's most prominent intellectuals. James' intelligence and capability ensured his heady ascent through a Trinity College, Dublin fellowship (where he was also one of its first and finest students), the bishopric of Meath, finally to acquire the mitre of archbishop of Armagh (and therefore head of the Church of Ireland), also taking a seat on the privy council. With a pedigree such as this, it is perhaps no surprise that Lewis and Mabel's eldest son Henry would also enter the Church.[5]

Henry Jones was born in 1605, and enrolled as a student of Trinity College, Dublin in 1616, receiving his B.A. degree in 1621. He then took an M.A., graduating in 1624. Jones obviously impressed during his time in Trinity, both as an undergraduate and postgraduate, as he was appointed to a fellowship there in the same year he received his M.A. The following year, 1625, Jones' father, Lewis, granted Henry the deanery of Ardagh diocese, which took in most of south Leitrim, Longford and also a part of Cavan. In

---

[2] See the losses which Jones recorded in his deposition: TCD, MS 840, fo. 32v.
[3] TCD, MS 840, fo. 32v.
[4] J.B. Leslie and D.W.T. Crooks, *Clergy of Kilmore, Elphin and Ardagh* (Belfast, 2008), p. 574.
[5] As did another son, Ambrose, who served as bishop of Kildare from 1667–9: Leslie & Crooks, *Clergy of Kilmore, Elphin & Ardagh*, p. 574.

1622, it was noted that Lewis Jones, Henry's father, had been granted 'three cartrons[6] of land lying near Ardagh' ... 'for three lives, with reservation of £3 16s. 8d. sterling *per annum*. The land may well be set for £18 sterling *per annum*'.[7] Lewis was not living there at the time, the deanery instead being served by a preacher named Thomas Mayot, but the deanery was noted to own 'good Irish houses', although the church was 'not well repaired'. Nevertheless, the deanery was worth £34 per annum, a tidy sum.[8]

In the ensuing years, Henry was granted a number of further positions, including the prebendary of Drom (1630–37), before entering Kilmore benefices, including the vicarage of Killeshandra (1631–33), and finally in 1637, the vicarages of Kildrumferton, Ballintemple and Kilmore, the diocese of which he was then also made dean (1637–45).[9] Kilmore was a wealthier diocese than Ardagh and encompassed most of County Cavan and north Leitrim, as well as parts of Counties Fermanagh and Meath. The valuation of the united dioceses of Kilmore and Ardagh in 1622 was £200, but it was likely higher than that. That same year, the cathedral at Kilmore was reportedly 'newly built and repaired', the funds to do so being taken from £175 worth of recusancy fines.[10] Its Church of Ireland bishop at the time of Jones' appointment was William Bedell. Bedell was baptised in Essex on 14 January 1572, studied in Emmanuel College, Cambridge, and held a number of ecclesiastical posts before his appointment in 1607 as chaplain to Sir Henry Wotton, English ambassador to Venice, where he spent four years. He was made provost of Trinity College, Dublin in 1627 before his translation to the joint Church of Ireland bishoprics of Kilmore and Ardagh in 1629, divesting himself of Ardagh in 1633. Bedell was almost seventy years old in late 1641 when he was imprisoned on Clogh Oughter, where he and his fellow prisoners were exposed to the harsh elements. Upon his release in early 1642, his house now occupied by the Catholic bishop of Kilmore, Eugene McSweeney, Bedell took lodgings with

---

[6] A cartron was about thirty acres.
[7] TCD, MS 550, fo. 138.
[8] Ibid., fo. 155.
[9] Leslie & Crooks, *Clergy of Kilmore, Elphin & Ardagh*, p. 572.
[10] TCD, MS 550, fo. 143. For more on Kilmore at this time, see Liam Kelly, *The diocese of Kilmore, c.1100–1800* (Dublin, 2017), chapters 9–12; Alan Ford, 'The reformation in Kilmore before 1641' in Raymond Gillespie (ed.), *Cavan: essays on the history of an Irish county* (Dublin, 1995, 2nd ed., 2004), pp 73–98.

a Gaelic Irish Protestant minister called Denis Sheridan. There, his health broke and Bedell died on 7 February 1642.[11]

Nowadays, Bedell is best known for his translation of the Old Testament into Irish as part of his drive to convert the local Gaelic Irish population to Protestantism and is regarded as something of a saintly figure. But he was a litigious man (for example, he sued his predecessor's widow over grants made of church property), whose righteousness and unyielding morality made him enemies wherever he went, including among his own clergy in Kilmore.[12] Bedell also had a falling out with Archbishop James Ussher in 1630 over the bishop's perceived softness on Catholicism, and it is possible that the bishop may not have been thrilled to see the archbishop's nephew appear in the diocese in 1637.[13] Jones' predecessor in the post, however, was Nicholas Bernard, with whom Bedell had also had a difficult relationship, so it could be that the bishop was relieved to see anybody else in the post than one of his nemeses.[14] Nevertheless, Jones seems to have regarded Bedell highly, describing the bishop as 'one of the brightest lights of that Church, both for learning and a shining conversation, and in his constant diligence in the work of the ministry, a pattern to others'.[15] It has been claimed by Aidan Clarke, Jones' most recent biographer, that the dean admired Bedell's use of the Irish language as a tool of proselytisation and not only rescued the bishop's manuscript translation of the Old Testament in 1641 but devoted much of his time in the 1670s to having it published (which eventually occurred in 1685).[16] And following his appointment as vice-chancellor of Dublin University in 1646, Jones advocated for the

---

[11] *Oxford DNB*, s.v., 'William Bedell'. Recent work on Bedell, which includes biographical detail, includes John McCafferty, 'Venice in Cavan: the career of William Bedell, 1572–1642' in Brendan Scott (ed.), *Culture and society in early modern Breifne/Cavan* (Dublin, 2009), pp 173–87; Marc Caball, '"A star of the first magnitude": William Bedell (1571–1642), bishop of Kilmore and Gaelic culture' in Jonathan Cherry and Brendan Scott (eds), *Cavan: history & society* (Dublin, 2014), pp 173–98.

[12] Brendan Scott, 'Accusations against Murtagh King, 1638', *Archivium Hibernicum*, 65 (2012), pp 76–81; idem, *Cavan 1609–53: plantation, war and religion* (Dublin, 2007), pp 25–8; Terence McCaughey, *Dr Bedell and Mr King: the making of the Irish Bible* (Dublin, 2001).

[13] Elizabethanne Boran (ed.), *The correspondence of James Ussher, 1600–1656*, 3 vols (Dublin, 2015), ii, pp 488–94, 502–03, 533–08. My sincere thanks to Dr Boran for our conversations on this point.

[14] *DIB*, s.v., 'Nicholas Bernard'.

[15] See below, p. 49.

[16] *DIB*, s.v., 'Henry Jones'.

resumption of Irish language classes for the students which Bedell had introduced during his time as provost there in the late 1620s.[17]

As dean of Kilmore, Jones' official residence was at Togher, in the parish of Kilmore, not far from the cathedral. Jones himself, however, referred in 1642 to his main home as being in Ballinagh, which is a short distance from Kilmore, describing it variously as a 'house' and as a 'castle'.[18] Likely it was an enclosed bawn of some sort, but it is curious that Jones did not refer to Togher himself as being his homestead – indeed, he mentioned in a deposition statement both Togher and Ballinagh, implying that he stored goods in Togher, but lived in Ballinagh.[19] In 1622, the deanery of Kilmore was noted as being 'merely titular, [with] nothing belonging unto it but the bishop for the time being and made choice of any one of his clergy whom he thought fittest to give unto him the name and title of a dean'.[20] The position in 1637 had obviously developed enough in the intervening fifteen years for an upwardly-mobile man such as Jones to take the post. Indeed, when giving his own, undated, deposition, Jones stated his losses to have come to £3019 10s. This was made up of livestock, horses, corn, hay and turf, household goods, books and buildings, rents in arrear and annual rents, probably from the settlers and Gaelic Irish alike. The rents in themselves made up £1219 of this figure, which indicates the degree to which Jones had become a beneficiary of the Plantation project in County Cavan.[21]

## County Cavan

Cavan, one of the six planted counties under the Ulster Plantation, was the most southerly of the Ulster counties. Formerly the Gaelic lordship of East Breifne, under the rule of the O'Reilly clan, what we now know as County Cavan was shired under the Tudors in 1579, although it existed in name only until 1583, when Crown representatives began to be appointed there.[22] Cavan's position in the 'buffer-zone' between the Pale and the north and north west, meant that the county and its people had interests both in the Pale and Gaelic Ireland.[23]

---

[17] Ibid.
[18] TCD, MS 840, fo. 32v; see below, p. 39.
[19] TCD, MS 840, fo. 32v.
[20] TCD, MS 550, fo 143.
[21] TCD, MS 840, fo. 32v.
[22] Christopher Maginn, 'Elizabethan Cavan: the institutions of Tudor government' in Scott (ed.), *Culture and society in early modern Breifne/Cavan*, pp 69–84 at pp 74–5.
[23] Bernadette Cunningham, 'The anglicisation of East Breifne: the O'Reillys and the emergence of County Cavan' in Gillespie (ed.), *Cavan*, pp 51–72 at p. 51.

Despite the best efforts of the O'Reillys to resist Plantation, the move against them was implacable and by 1610, British men, women and children were settling in the county.[24] Made up of seven baronies, 56,500 acres were given over for Plantation in the county.[25] Of these baronies, Loughtee was granted to English undertakers, Scottish undertakers received Tullyhunco and Clankee, while the lands in Tullyhaw, Tullygarvey, Castlerahan and Clanmahon were distributed among servitors and native 'deserving' Irish, normally members of the O'Reilly clan.[26] But almost 22.5% of the total area given over to Plantation in Cavan (albeit generally poorer quality land) was granted to the native Irish, including 96.5% in Clanmahon.[27] The main towns established or planted in the county included Cavan town, Belturbet, Virginia, Killeshandra and Bailieborough. These did not all develop at the same pace, however, and Cavan town and Belturbet grew at a much quicker pace than did Virginia, for example. And despite the establishment of these towns, it was later noted by William Bedell's son and namesake that although Cavan was 'meetly well planted with English', it was done so 'scatteringly here and their which facilitated their ruin … [and] the Irish were more than five times their number and all of them obstinate papists'.[28] Jones also noted this in the *Relation*, writing how the British 'dwelt scatteringly'.[29] This lax attitude on the settlers' part regarding their security would have profound consequences in 1641 and the following years. But despite some threatened or actual civil unrest in the 1620s, there is also evidence of the settler and native communities working together as was the case in 1629, when famine and taxation saw them unify in protest at onerous exactions as part of what is known as the 'Graces'.[30]

---

[24] For more on this episode, see Ciaran Brady, 'The end of the O'Reilly lordship, 1584–1610' in David Edwards (ed.), *Regions and rulers in Ireland, 1100–1650: essays for Kenneth Nicholls* (Dublin, 2004), pp 174–200.

[25] Calculated from George Hill, *An historical account of the plantation in Ulster* (Belfast, 1877), p. 185.

[26] Scott, *Cavan 1609–1653*, p. 12.

[27] Robert J. Hunter, *The Ulster plantation in the counties of Armagh and Cavan, 1608–1641* (Belfast, 2012), p. 78; Brendan Scott, 'The Ulster plantation and its effect on native and settler in Cavan, 1610–41' in Cherry and Scott (eds), *Cavan: history and society*, pp 149–72 at p. 153.

[28] E.S. Shuckburgh (ed.), *Two biographies of William Bedell, bishop of Kilmore* (Cambridge, 1902), pp 56–7.

[29] See below, p. 35.

[30] See Brendan Scott, 'Select document: "Petition of the inhabitants of Cavan to the lord deputy and council", 8 July 1629', *Irish Historical Studies*, 43:163 (2019), pp 111–25; David Edwards, 'Out of the blue? Provincial unrest in Ireland

That same year, a total of 838 adult male British settlers appeared for muster in County Cavan, giving some indication of the county's settler population almost twenty years into the plantation project. Of this figure, 420 were mustered in Loughtee barony, with a further 27 mustering in Cavan town, and 210 in Tullyhunco barony. None mustered at all in Tullyhaw, Clanmahon or Tullygarvey baronies.[31] Twelve years later, however, the 1641 rising took place, which had devastating consequences for the British settlers throughout Ireland.[32]

The political climate in the kingdoms of England and Wales, Scotland and Ireland had deteriorated as the 1630s drew to a close. King Charles I, who was married to a French Catholic and was regarded by his Catholic subjects as their traditional defender, was under severe pressure from Westminster's ever-strengthening puritan parliament. Looking on with concern at this move against the king was a group of Catholic landowners which coalesced around Rory O'More, who held a Plantation estate in Armagh. O'More approached Conor Maguire, the second Lord Enniskillen, and convinced him to support a military show of force against the government in Ireland. By 1641, Maguire was the largest single landowner in Fermanagh, with holdings amounting to a total of 22,351 acres, yet was heavily indebted and in danger of losing his estates. Maguire in turn persuaded Sir Phelim O'Neill, MP for Dungannon, to support the venture. The plan devised by O'More, O'Neill and Maguire involved bringing 200 men into Dublin on Saturday 23 October, which was a market day. Led by Maguire and O'More, this force of men would take Dublin Castle. Concurrently, the plan went, an uprising in Ulster led by Phelim O'Neill would take place, its aim the seizing of various strategic castles and bases. But before the planned attack on Dublin Castle could take place, however, the plot was betrayed, and Maguire and O'More were arrested without the rising in Dublin ever actually getting off the ground.[33]

---

before 1641' in Micheál Ó Siochrú and Jane Ohlmeyer (eds), *Ireland 1641: contexts and reactions* (Manchester, 2013), pp 95–114; *Cal. S.P. Ire., 1625–32*, pp 35–7, 220.

[31] Calculated from Robert J. Hunter and John Johnston (eds), *'Men and arms': the Ulster settlers, c.1630* (Belfast, 2012), pp 2–16.

[32] For an excellent recent essay on the historiography of 1641, see Brian Mac Cuarta, 'Ulster 1641: a select bibliography, 1993–2018' in Brian Mac Cuarta (ed.), *Ulster 1641: aspects of the rising* (3rd ed., Belfast, 2020), pp vi–xxii.

[33] Pádraig Lenihan, *Consolidating conquest: Ireland, 1603–1727* (Harlow, 2008), pp 91–3; Raymond Gillespie, *Seventeenth-century Ireland* (Dublin, 2006), p. 141; TCD, MS 809, fos 24r–25v.

Unaware of what had happened in Dublin, the rising in Ulster led by O'Neill did take place, however, but quickly spiralled out of control. Various elements of native Irish society, unhappy with the plantation process and their reduced status within it, and who were suffering from the challenging economic circumstances of the 1620s and 1630s, hijacked the rising and it became instead an opportunity for those disaffected to address their grievances. Very soon, large numbers of British settlers and their families were being expelled from their houses, robbed and stripped of their clothes, and some attacked and killed, the remainder trudging through the snow and frost which was reported by many of the settlers, to the safety of the Pale and its towns, in particular Dublin. Three of the Plantation towns in County Cavan, Cavan town, Belturbet and Killeshandra, appear in Jones' *Relation* and he reports what happened in these towns during the initial months of the rising.

## Cavan town

The Plantation process in Cavan was perhaps not the culture shock as it may have been in other areas due to the commercial interactions of the O'Reillys with the Pale and the garrisoning of English soldiers in the town during the Nine Years' War.[34] Built up around the Franciscan friary which was established in the early fourteenth century,[35] the town continued to develop when the O'Reillys established their centre there on Tullymongan Hill.[36] Located as it was close to the Pale in the barony of Loughtee, Cavan had a long history of trading with the Englishry and its position as a Gaelic market town was almost unique in Ireland. The O'Reillys also allied themselves with the Dublin administration on occasion, hemmed in as they were by the O'Neill, Maguire, O'Rourke and MacMahon clans. Cavan town was destroyed or burned at least three times between 1429 and 1576, and witnessed further destruction in 1641 and again in 1690 during the Williamite War.[37] The devastation wrought upon the town at various

---

[34] Cunningham, 'The anglicisation of East Breifne', p. 71.
[35] There is some uncertainty as to the date of the friary's establishment: Kelly, *The diocese of Kilmore*, pp 62–3.
[36] See Jonathan Cherry, 'The indigenous and colonial urbanization of Cavan town, c. 1300–c. 1641' in Scott (ed.), *Culture and society in early modern Breifne/Cavan*, pp 85–105.
[37] Jonathan Cherry and Brendan Scott, 'Cavan town: an overview' in Brendan Scott (ed.), *Cavan town, 1610–2010: a brief history* (Cavan, 2012), pp 1–18 at p. 1; Brendan Scott, 'Accounts of the battle of Cavan town, 1690' in Scott (ed.), *Cavan town*, pp 19–27.

points led Sir Arthur Chichester, the lord deputy, to comment in 1606 that Cavan was a 'poor town ... seated betwixt many small hills'.[38]

The famous map of the town from the 1590s gives us some idea of what Cavan may have looked like at this time, even taking into account some possible artistic licence on the part of the cartographer.[39] The market cross, located at the centre of the town, indicates where the markets and fairs would have been held, overlooked by the O'Reilly castle (noted as 'Aurelies castell') at Tullymongan. The abbey, around which the town coalesced, is also clearly visible in the corner of the map (which is in itself part of a larger map of Fermanagh and Cavan). Some of the other buildings likely include a gaol, court house and school, which were agreed to be constructed by Sir John O'Reilly upon the shiring of the county in 1579.[40]

In November 1610, Cavan was granted a charter from James I, the first town under the Ulster Plantation scheme to receive one.[41] The make-up of its first corporation was quite Gaelic in character, with its first sovereign (mayor), named as Walter Brady, who had been appointed gaoler of the town in 1584.[42] There were references in 1641 to Irishmen living in the town and to the gaoler, one 'Patrick O Rely'.[43] Only three English names were listed in the charter of 1610, including Hugh Culme, Henry Jones' future father-in-law. The abbey was to become the parish church for the Church of Ireland, and also became the site of a free school established for the children of the planters. The church was described as ruinous in 1622 and it was recommended that a new church be built in its place, although this did not happen.[44] Although Cavan was made the county town, Belturbet was actually reckoned by the 1630s to be twice the size of Cavan.[45] By 1641, the then sovereign of the town, Stephen Allen, was living in the 'Abby of Cavan', but by early November, the town had fallen and Allen was ejected from the premises.[46]

---

[38] *Cal. S.P. Ire., 1603–06*, p. 565; G.A. Hayes-McCoy, 'Sir John Davies in Cavan in 1606 and 1610', *Breifne*, 3 (1960), pp 171–91 at p. 183.

[39] TNA, MPF 1/81.

[40] Cherry and Scott, 'Cavan town', p. 2.

[41] For a text of the charter, see Jonathan Cherry, 'The 1610 Cavan town charter: an introduction and transcription', *Breifne*, 45 (2009–10), pp 1–12.

[42] *Cal. S.P. Ire., 1509–73*, p. 646.

[43] TCD, MS 832, fo. 174v. Cavan's gaol was noted in the early seventeenth century for its poor conditions: Liam Kelly, 'Prisons and punishments in County Cavan, 1600–1800', *Breifne*, 55 (2020), pp 597–605.

[44] TCD, MS 550, fo. 147.

[45] Shuckburgh (ed.), *Two biographies of William Bedell*, p. 57.

[46] TCD, MS 832, fo. 174r.

## Belturbet

Belturbet, granted to the English undertaker Stephen Butler, was officially established as a Plantation town on 18 July 1610. Earlier settlements here had centred around an Anglo-Norman motte and bailey and a sixteenth-century O'Reilly castle on the shore of the River Erne.[47] Unlike the proposed settlement at what was to become Virginia, County Cavan, the settlement was quickly underway and the town was soon thriving.[48] In the spring of 1611, Butler, who was granted 2,000 acres in Loughtee barony, had appointed a deputy and installed twelve to sixteen men on his estate; by that autumn, he had planted forty-one families in Belturbet and its hinterland.[49] Belturbet received its charter in 1613, with Butler appointed what the charter referred to as 'chief officer', or, as it was known elsewhere, provost, and a report that year stated that the corporation 'goeth well forward',[50] and in 1618/19, there were a number of 'houses built of cage-work all inhabited with British tenants, and most of them tradesmen, each of these having a house and garden plot, with four acres of land, and commons for certain numbers of cows and garrons'.[51] Building projects initiated by Butler (who was now based in Clonosey, outside the town) had continued apace, and two corn mills and a fulling mill on his estate were recorded in Pynnar's survey of the plantation in 1618–19. A further survey of Ireland took place in 1622, which also investigated the progress of the Plantation in Ulster. The commissioners reported that by that year, Butler had built thirty-four houses in Belturbet, employing bricklayers, carpenters and smiths to construct them, and it is estimated that there were probably about 170 people resident there. Bishop William Bedell's son and namesake remarked that Belturbet was the 'only considerable town in the whole county' and that Cavan town itself 'was not so big by one half as Belterbert', a sentiment seconded by Henry Jones, who noted that the town was 'the most populous, and of all others the best English plantation in that

---

[47] Brendan Scott, *Belturbet, County Cavan, 1610–1714: the origins of an Ulster plantation town* (Dublin, 2020), p. 9.

[48] Robert J. Hunter, 'An Ulster Plantation town: Virginia', *Breifne*, 4 (1970), pp 43–51; Raymond Gillespie, 'Plantation Virginia revisited', *Breifne*, 49 (2014), pp 302–14; *Cal. pat. rolls Ire., Jas I*, p. 423; Scott, *Belturbet, County Cavan, 1610–1714*, pp 9–11.

[49] Robert J. Hunter, 'The English undertakers in the Plantation of Ulster [*recte* Cavan], 1610–41', *Breifne*, 16 (1973–5), pp 471–99 at p. 478; F. Bickley (ed.), *Historical Manuscripts Commission: report on the manuscripts of the late Reginald Rawdon Hastings Esq. of the Manor House, Ashby de la Zouch* (London, 1947), iv, p. 163.

[50] Bickley (ed.), *HMC, Hastings MSS*, iv, p. 163.

[51] Hill, *An historical account*, pp 465–6.

country'.[52] In 1634, Belturbet was described as 'a comfortable place for residence' and the rectory was reckoned to be worth at least £300 annually.[53]

But all of this development and growth came to a halt in October 1641, upon the beginning of the rising that year. Although there was a small garrison of troops in Belturbet, there were no defensive walls there and the faltering attempt made by Captain Richard Ryves and his men to defend the town against the Irish insurgents soon ended in failure. It was reported afterward in the form of a deposition that:

> Phillip mc Hugh ô Rely, Phillip Mulmore ô Rely, & Mulmore ô Rely with other of theire followers sent word to the towne of Belturbat that vnles they would yeald vnto them the towne with all there weapons and municion, they wold come & destroy the towne and all the inhabitants with fier and sword.[54]

Given their lack of defences, it was no surprise that the people of Belturbet resolved to surrender to Philip MacHugh O'Reilly, even though Jones notes that they were advised not to do so by another planter, Sir Francis Hamilton.[55] Following this resolution to lay down arms, Ryves and his men departed for Cavan town.[56] Most of the settlers in Belturbet were attacked and ejected from their homes from 1 November onwards.[57] Although most settlers were permitted (or forced) to leave Belturbet some of those with trades were forced to remain in the town and serve the Irish. But by around the end of January 1642, over thirty Planter men, women and children still in Belturbet were either hanged or drowned in the River Erne by the Gaelic Irish. Two men, Timothy Dickson and Raphe Carr, were hanged at the Diamond,[58] following which, the others were led to the river, where they were drowned. At least thirty-five British deponents who survived the rising gave Belturbet as their address, so Jones would have had plenty of information coming from the town and what had happened there, although, not yet having access to the two eyewitness reports of the massacre

---

[52] Shuckburgh (ed.), *Two biographies of William Bedell*, p. 57; see below, p. 36.
[53] *Cal. S.P. Ire., 1633–47*, p. 88.
[54] TCD, MS 833, fo. 34r.
[55] See below, p. 37.
[56] TCD, MS 833, fos 115v, 174v.
[57] See for example, TCD, MS 833, fos 148r, 225r, 256r and many of the depositions given by Belturbet deponents.
[58] TCD, MS 833, fos 249r–v.

which were eventually given to the commission in 1643 and 1652, he offered in the *Relation* the higher and unsubstantiated figure of sixty dead.[59]

## Killeshandra

Killeshandra, in the barony of Tullyhunco, was planted by the Hamiltons, a Scottish planter family, one of whom, Francis, will be discussed in more detail below. The entire barony of Tullyhunco was given over to Scottish planters and by 1622, it was reported that there were twenty houses inhabited by British families in Killeshandra. But all was not well there, and the settlers complained to the commissioners employed that year to survey the state and progress of the plantation that 'they have been at great charge in building and planting themselves there upon promise of certain freehold estates to be made to them'. But as Claud Hamilton, the original grantee was dead, and his son, Francis, was still a minor, this issue had not been resolved satisfactorily.[60] But the problem must have been settled in some way, as by 1629, the town had grown and there were now thirty-four houses there, all peopled with British settlers in 'English-like houses' and where the fairs and markets were held.[61] In 1631, Francis Hamilton was granted a patent which declared that the dates of Killeshandra's markets and fairs be altered for the convenience of the inhabitants in the area; presumably the dates clashed with another town or village nearby, although a case regarding the ownership of the townland in which Killeshandra's markets were held had dragged on in chancery between 1614–25.[62] There had been moves to restore Killeshandra's church and in 1622 it was reported that the church there had been 'newly repaired'.[63] But all of these developments literally went up in flames when Hamilton torched the town in 1642 rather than allow it to fall into the hands of the Gaelic insurgents, as had happened in Belturbet and Cavan. Together, Francis Hamilton and James Craig offered the only significant British resistance to the Gaelic Irish insurgents during these initial months of the rising.

---

[59] See the depositions of William Gibbs and Peter Rickarbee which were given in 1643 and 1654 respectively: TCD, MS 833, fos 249r–50v, 295r–96v. See below, p. 55.

[60] Victor Treadwell (ed.), *The Irish commission of 1622: an investigation of the Irish administration 1615–22 and its consequences 1623–24* (Dublin, 2006), p. 520.

[61] Hunter, *The Ulster plantation*, p. 172; *Inquisitionum in officio rotulorum cancellariae Hiberniae asservatarum repertorium*, ii (Dublin, 1829), Cavan, 24 Car. I.

[62] Hunter, *The Ulster plantation*, pp 282–3.

[63] TCD, MS 550, fo. 151; Oliver Davies, 'The churches of County Cavan' in *R.S.A.I. Jn.*, 78: (1948), pp 73–118 (reprinted in *Breifne*, 48 (2013), pp 90–145 at p. 115).

## Francis Hamilton

Francis Hamilton and James Craig, two Scottish undertakers in the precinct of Tullyhunco, both play an important part in Jones' *Relation*, as the only two settlers to resist in any meaningful way the insurgents and their activities. Francis' family had arrived in Cavan at the beginning of the Ulster Plantation when his grandfather, Sir Alexander Hamilton of Innerwick, was granted 2,000 acres in Tullyhunco, as well as the advowson for the church at Killeshandra, which lies in that barony. Alexander never seems to have settled in in Tullyhunco, or perhaps even visited, and he left it to his son Claud.[64] It was reported in in 1613 that the 'performance of the conditions [of plantation] is undertaken by Claud Hamilton ... who doth very effectually intend and follow the same'.[65] But the following year, Claud was dead and although the estate still belonged to Alexander, in 1621, he granted it to his grandson Francis. While still a minor, the estate was managed by his mother Jane and his stepfather Sir Arthur Forbes from Aberdeenshire, who had received lands in Longford and Leitrim under the Plantation scheme there.[66]

Francis came from an influential family, and following his majority he inherited his father's property in Scotland, was made a member of the Scottish privy council, created a baronet, granted 16,000 acres in Nova Scotia and elected an MP for Jamestown in County Leitrim in 1639. Francis married a daughter of Sir Charles Coote, a prominent (and notorious) English settler who owned ironworks in Doobally in West Cavan.[67] Both the Hamiltons and James Craig built their bawns[68] in Keelagh and Croghan close to one another, separated by only about one

---

[64] William Roulston, 'The Scots in Plantation Cavan' in Scott (ed.), *Culture and society in early modern Breifne/Cavan*, pp 121–46 at pp 123–4.

[65] HMC, *Hastings MSS*, iv, p. 164.

[66] Forbes was later killed in a duel by Sir Frederick Hamilton (no relation of Francis) of Manorhamilton while serving in Germany during the Thirty Years' War: Dominic Rooney, *The life and times of Sir Frederick Hamilton, 1590–1647* (Dublin, 2013), p. 63; Shuckburgh (ed.), *Two biographies of William Bedell*, p. 195. This probably explains the presence of Arthur Forbes' son and namesake in Keelagh in 1642 (although his mother was at the family's castle in Longford): Shuckburgh (ed.), *Two lives of William Bedell*, pp 195, 212; see below, p. 59.

[67] Roulston, 'The Scots in Plantation Cavan', p. 124; Kevin Forkan, 'Inventing an Irish Protestant icon: the strange death of Sir Charles Coote, 1642' in David Edwards, Pádraig Lenihan and Clodagh Tait (eds), *Age of atrocity: violence and political conflict in early modern Ireland* (Dublin, 2007), pp 204–218; Shuckburgh (ed.), *Two biographies of William Bedell*, p. 195.

[68] Fortified houses were often referred to as castles in contemporary records.

mile of 'woody ground', probably for reasons of defence.[69] William Bedell's biographer, Alexander Clogy, recorded that Hamilton and Craig had built their castles (which he called 'arks'), 'being moved with fear and prudence … for the safety of their respective families'.[70] If this was indeed the case, it certainly was a wise move, as later events would prove.

In 1613, Josias Bodley, who was tasked by the king to survey the progress of the Ulster Plantation, noted that the Hamiltons had at Keelagh:

> built a stone house of exceeding good strength, on all parts well flanked, being about 60 feet in length and 22 in breadth, which is already raised to the sole of the window of the third story.[71]

The bawn, which was not yet completed, was made of lime and stone and reckoned to be 'strongly built'. The castle was described in 1622 as 'a very strong bawn of stone and lime with 4 flankers, and within it a strong castle, 4 storeys high, long since finished'.[72] Hamilton's castle in Keelagh was described in an inquisition dating from 1629[73] which gives us a very good idea of the building's size and layout. The castle was said to be made of lime and stone, four storeys high, with 'flankers and turrets for the better defence thereof'.[74] The castle seems to have survived the siege which Jones describes in the *Relation* and was noted in 1664 as having six hearths, but seems to have been destroyed during the Williamite Wars and rebuilt by the early eighteenth century.[75] Following his departure from Cavan in 1642, Hamilton continued to play an active role in public life. In 1644, he was appointed commander of Colonel Chichester's regiment and troop of horse and, along with others, raised twelve troops of horse in Ireland in 1648. In 1646, Hamilton's company travelled to Scotland, from whence in 1649, he took part in the duke of Hamilton's 1649 expedition into England for which he was censured in 1651 and which he apologised for. Hamilton returned to

---

[69] Alexander Clogy, *Memoir of the life and episcopate of Dr William Bedell*, ed. W.W. Wilkins (London, 1862), p. 214. In 1631, it was discovered that two polls of land belonging to Hamilton had been 'wrongfullie held and possessed' by Craig, which must have been a source of tension between the two men: Hunter, *The Ulster plantation*, p. 172.

[70] Clogy, *Memoir of the life and episcopate of Dr William Bedell*, p. 173.

[71] HMC, *Hastings MSS*, iv, p. 164.

[72] Treadwell (ed.), *The Irish commission of 1622*, p. 520.

[73] *Inquisitionum in officio rotulorum*, ii, Cavan, 24 Car. I.

[74] Oliver Davies, 'The castles of County Cavan, part II', *Ulster Journal of Archaeology*, 3rd series, 11 (1948), pp 81–126 (reprinted in *Breifne*, 48 (2013), pp 43–89 at p. 78).

[75] Ibid.

Cavan and Castle Hamilton some time after this and was appointed justice of the peace for the county in 1661. He also served as an MP again, this time for the county, from 1651 to 1666. Francis survived his first wife and married Elizabeth Barlow, the daughter of Randall Barlow, archbishop of Tuam. Francis died in 1673, leaving five children born to his first wife.[76]

## James Craig

James Craig appeared in Tullyhunco in 1611 as the estate agent of the Aghmootie brothers who had been granted land in Dromheada and Keelagh.[77] Very quickly they sold their interest to Craig, who had by 1611 built a castle, which in 1613 was reckoned to be very similar to that of Francis Hamilton (see above), although Craig also had built a platform designed to hold two small cannon.[78] That year, it was noted that Craig's house or castle was 'ready for the roof' and that the bawn was 'very near at the full height'. Craig was also 'well provided of arms' and had about twelve tenants in place. At the time of Bodley's Survey of 1613, Craig was in England, attempting to attract more settlers to his estate.[79] In Pynnar's survey of 1618–19, it was noted that Craig's castle was 'twenty feet broad and five storeys high'. The bawn itself was recorded as being seventy-five feet square, sixteen feet high, with four round towers acting as flankers.[80] Craig's base was again described in 1622, when, along with a stable and other buildings within the perimeter walls, the bawn itself was noted as being:

> Of stone and lime, 83 foot long, 46 foot broad, 12 foot high, besides 4 large round towers for flankers at each corner. Within the said bawn there is also built a strong castle of stone and lime, 60 foot long and 20 foot broad, within the walls, 4 storeys and a half high.[81]

An inquisition from 1629 notes the castle's dimensions to be '35 feet in height, within a circuit or enclosure of 240 feet in circumference'.[82] Part of this castle survives – the south-west corner of the bawn, complete with slits

---

[76] George Hamilton, *A history of the House of Hamilton* (Edinburgh, 1933), pp 499–500. My sincere thanks to Dr William Roulston for sharing this source with me.

[77] For more on the townlands which made up this estate, see Maura Nallen's excellent article, 'A study of eight townlands in the parish of Killeshandra, 1608–1841', *Breifne*, 35 (1999), pp 5–84.

[78] Hunter, *The Ulster plantation*, p. 121.

[79] Bickley (ed.), *HMC, Hastings MSS*, iv, p. 164.

[80] Hill, *Plantation of Ulster*, p. 471.

[81] Treadwell (ed.), *The Irish commission of 1622*, p. 521.

[82] Hill, *Plantation of Ulster*, p. 471.

and a first-floor door on to the wall walk. It is built with small stones, circular in shape and with an inside diameter of ten foot. Still visible in the 1940s were banks which marked the location of the walls of the bawn itself – the south and east walls were noted by Oliver Davies to have been on the brow of a 'fairly steep slope to the river'.[83] Davies also discerned at this time a corbelled chamber opening into a slab-roofed passage which was located to the north-west of the west wall, which he believed may have been a 'secret exit or a well-chamber'.[84] This flanker still exists.[85]

It is likely that Craig was from Edinburgh, and was one of the coterie who travelled south to London with the new king, James I, in 1603. He received a number of royal appointments and in 1610 was granted 1,000 acres in Armagh. Craig grew in importance as a representative of Scottish and planter interests in Ireland and soon was acquiring land across Ireland, from Mayo to Waterford, receiving 1,000 acres in Leitrim as part of the plantation process there in the 1620s, and serving as sheriff of Cavan in 1615.[86] He created further connections for himself through his marriage to a daughter of Moses Hill, an English planter based near Belfast.[87] But in the 1620s, Craig's tenants (he had twenty-one British families on his estate) complained that they had no official leases for their properties, rather 'promises or short notes under Sir James his hand'. Perhaps for that reason, not all tenants were present on their lands and rather had sublet to native Irish instead.[88] That same year, it was noted that Craig held weapons in his bawn, including muskets, calivers, swords and pistols, as well as thirty pikes and halfpikes.[89] Craig was also appointed in the 1630s to a commission intended to plan the town of Virginia and an intended corporation there.[90]

Once the rising broke out, Hamilton and Craig 'fortified [their castles] for their lives', opening them up to British settlers fleeing their homes in fear of their lives. Alexander Clogy describes how the settlers 'made huts and cabins within and without the barn [sic] walls [Craig and Hamilton's bawns], and covered them with cowhides'.[91] Although they had some

---

[83] Davies, 'The castles of County Cavan, part II', p. 78.

[84] Ibid., pp 78–9.

[85] A photograph of it dating from *c.* 2010 can be seen on the back cover of Tomás Ó Raghallaigh, *Turbulence in Tullyhunco* (Cavan, 2010). My thanks to Tomás for his discussions on this point.

[86] Roulston, 'The Scots in Plantation Cavan', pp 125–6; RIA, Upton MS 19a.

[87] Roulston, 'The Scots in Plantation Cavan', p. 126.

[88] Treadwell (ed.), *The Irish commission of 1622*, pp 521–22.

[89] Ibid., p. 522.

[90] Hunter, *The Ulster plantation*, p. 251.

[91] Clogy, *Memoir of the life and episcopate of Dr William Bedell*, p. 214.

initial successes in their forays from Keelagh and Croghan against the Irish, the siege conditions soon began to tell, and by the summer of 1642, the outlook was bleak for those within their walls, with settlers forced to eat the cow hides which covered their huts. Starvation and sickness, exacerbated by the cramped conditions, led to a significant loss of life among the settlers, with Craig dying at this time, to be buried at the church in Killeshandra. But we do have some further information regarding what has been termed the 'strange afterlife' of James Craig. According to Ambrose Bedell, a son of the bishop, Craig's

> corps were taken up out of the grave by the Rebells and cutt in peecs And they after they had taken away his coffin and sheete & had soe hact and mangled him they threw his mangled bodie into the grave againe.[92]

The timber from the coffin and the shroud in which he had been wrapped would have been valuable commodities in and of themselves. This story is not mentioned anywhere else, but it may be that Craig's active resistance of the rebellion had made him unpopular among the rebels, hence the desecration of his remains.[93] Craig's loss was felt keenly by Henry Jones, who wrote of him in the *Relation* that the Scottish planter was a 'gentleman of singular and the best abilities; well deserving of his country both in peace and war: of whom I say the less because I cannot write enough'.[94] But how did other families connected with Jones fare throughout this period?

## The Culme family

Henry Jones' first wife was Jane, daughter of a Cavan planter, Hugh Culme.[95] The Culme family, originally from Devon, appeared in Ireland before the Ulster Plantation began, and a brother of Hugh's named Benjamin, was dean of St Patrick's Cathedral in Dublin, but the family quickly became beneficiaries of the new Plantation of Cavan.[96] In early 1610, Arthur Chichester recommended that Captain Hugh Culme receive

---

[92] TCD, MS 833, fo. 105v. It is important to note that Bedell does not seem to have witnessed this himself; rather, he was reporting hearsay.
[93] Brendan Scott, 'The strange burials and "afterlives" of William Bedell and James Craig' in Salvador Ryan (ed.), *Death and the Irish: a miscellany* (Dublin, 2016), pp 75–77.
[94] See below, p. 56.
[95] *D.I.B.*, s.v., Henry Jones'.
[96] Brian C. Donovan and David Edwards, *British sources for Irish history, 1485–1641: a guide to manuscripts in local, regional and specialised repositories in England, Scotland and Wales* (Dublin, 1997), p. 41.

lands in Cavan as a servitor.[97] Culme was already constable of Clogh Oughter castle and he received it, along with its lands in a twenty-one year lease in November of that year.[98] It was a productive year for Culme, as he was also appointed provost-marshal of County Cavan for 1610.[99] Culme was also granted lands along with Walter Talbot in the barony of Tullyhaw in West Cavan, where in the first years of the Plantation, they had built a strong timber house, two wattled houses and had felled forty trees. By 1613, they had built '3 or 4 handsome Irish houses' there, possibly the origins of the town of Ballyconnell.[100] Culme also engaged in a similar joint project with Archibald Moore in Tullygarvey barony, establishing a settlement in Tullyvin, a partnership which ended by 1618/19 upon the death of Moore.[101]

Culme quickly took a leading role in the leadership of the county, and served as sheriff for the county from 1612 to 1613.[102] He was also a member of Cavan's first corporation and was elected MP for County Cavan in the election held in 1613. This result was strongly protested by the Gaelic Irish of Cavan with the result that he and George Sexton (the other Protestant candidate), were deselected and replaced with their opponents, Walter and Thomas Brady.[103] That Culme and both Bradys were members

[97] Hunter, *The Ulster plantation*, p. 47.
[98] Clogh Oughter is a circular castle with extensive damage situated on an island in Lough Oughter. What survives now was probably begun by the Anglo-Norman de Lacy family in the early thirteenth century. The O'Reillys took possession of it in the thirteenth century and it became initially their headquarters but eventually a prison. It was granted to the Culme family in the early seventeenth century but was retaken by the Gaelic Irish in 1641, when it became a prison, with one of its most famous occupants being Bishop William Bedell, who was held there in December and January 1641–2. It was the site of Eoghan Roe O'Neill's death in 1649 and was besieged by Commonwealth forces in March 1653. Following its capitulation in late April that year (the last major fortified Confederacy position in Ireland to do so), it was destroyed by the Commonwealth forces, led by Theophilus Jones, a brother of Henry's. For more on Clogh Oughter, see the excellent survey of the site by Conleth Manning, *Clogh Oughter Castle, County Cavan: archaeology, history and architecture* (Dublin, 2013).
[99] Hunter, *The Ulster plantation*, p. 55.
[100] Originally granted to Culme alone, the land in Tullyhaw was owned outright by Talbot's son by the time of Culme's death in 1630: Hunter, *The Ulster plantation*, pp 56, 72, 93.
[101] Hunter, *The Ulster plantation*, p. 152.
[102] RIA, Upton MS, 19a.
[103] Bríd McGrath, 'Unconstitutional acts, violence, intimidation, vote-rigging, fraud and resistance: Cavan's parliamentary elections, 1613', *Breifne* (forthcoming, 2021).

of Cavan town's corporation must have led to awkwardness afterwards. Yet this setback did not deter Culme and he served as provost-marshal of Cavan and Monaghan from 1617–19.[104] He continued to provide a leadership role in Cavan and reported to Dublin in 1623 a group of friars which assembled in Cavan town, attended by, according to Culme at least, 2,000 people.[105] In 1629, Culme, along with just over 100 others in Cavan, both British settler and Gaelic Irish alike, signed a letter of protest against onerous 'Grace' payments due to the Crown which were to be paid at a time of recession and famine in Ireland, Culme's being one of the first signatures appended to the letter.[106]

By 1619, Culme had bought Captain John Ridgeway's interest in what was to become the town of Virginia, which finally began to develop under his supervision.[107] He also provided a preacher for the town; it has been suggested that this may have been Hugh's brother, Benjamin, although it seems to have been George Creighton.[108] In 1620, Hugh was once again leased Clogh Oughter and its lands for another twenty-one year period, and also received leases of church lands in Kilmore diocese from the Church of Ireland bishop there.[109] Indeed, his acquisitiveness was such that having begun the Plantation process with roughly 4,500 acres in Cavan, by 1641 his son Arthur, along with other members of the family, had amassed between them around 12,000 acres, although he did sell his interest in Virginia to the earl of Fingall in 1622.[110] Hugh's brother Benjamin, for example, although dean of St Patrick's Cathedral in Dublin, also held lands in Cavan and had also bought property belonging to a relative named Philip Culme in the barony of Loughtee in the 1630s.[111] Hugh died in 1630 and was succeeded by his son Arthur.[112]

Arthur Culme, who was based at Clogh Oughter, swiftly adopted his father's mantle as one of Cavan's political leaders and was appointed in

---

[104] *Cal. S.P. Ire., 1615–25*, pp 194–96, 245–47.

[105] Ibid., pp 432–3.

[106] Scott, 'Select document: "Petition of the inhabitants of Cavan to the lord deputy and council", 8 July 1629'. Culme also set his signature to a second letter on this matter, this one from 'the knights and gentlemen of Ireland': TNA, SP 63/249, fos 17–18.

[107] Hunter, 'An Ulster plantation town', pp 43–51. Culme was absent in 1622 when Virginia was surveyed, although his wife and family were present: Treadwell (ed.), *The Irish commission of 1622*, p. 513.

[108] Hill, *Plantation of Ulster*, p. 458; Hunter, *The Ulster plantation*, p. 124.

[109] *Cal. pat. rolls Ire., Jas I*, p. 461; Hunter, *The Ulster plantation*, p. 313n.

[110] Hunter, *The Ulster plantation*, p. 380; idem, 'Virginia', p. 49.

[111] Hunter, *The Ulster plantation*, p. 193; Donovan and Edwards, *British sources for Irish history*, pp 44–45.

[112] Donovan and Edwards, *British sources for Irish history*, p. 258.

1636 to a commission established to enquire into leases of episcopal property in Kilmore, which is ironic given that his father benefitted from ecclesiastical leases at the expense of the Church.[113] He also undertook land improvements on his properties (which included forty polls of land in Monaghan), as in 1642, it was reported that he owed two deponents 40*s*. for draining a bog prior to the uprising.[114]

Understanding the strategic importance of Clogh Oughter, on the first day of the rising, the Gaelic Irish insurgents took possession of the castle and imprisoned Arthur, his wife Mary, who had recently given birth, and one of his children (not the new-born infant, but his eldest son) on the island.[115] Coming to his house in Inishconnell townland on the shore of Lough Oughter, the rebels demanded that Culme hand over the key to the castle, which Culme described as a 'comfortless' but 'stronge tower'.[116] Culme refused, leading the rebels to threaten his life, upon which a relation of his named Anthony Culme, who had the key, offered to bring it to them in exchange for Arthur's life. The rebels also took possession of Culme's house and used it as a central base to store corn and money.[117] Culme, his wife and child were held on the island from late October 1641 and were joined for roughly one month beginning in mid-December by a party which included Bishop William Bedell. This group, which did not include Culme's entourage, was later released following an exchange of prisoners organised by James Craig.[118] In early 1642, a number of priests and friars visited Culme and attempted to persuade him to renounce Protestantism and embrace Catholicism. If he were to do that, the clergy claimed, Culme's money and lands would be restored to him; Culme refused. The rest of Culme's family fared little better; indeed, one of his children died, possibly from exposure, while the rest in May 1642 were 'sent to Irish Cottes liveing on the Almes of Irish Bagares, And 2 of them still amongst them'.[119] Around 23 April that year, Culme, his wife and son were released as part of a prisoner exchange agreement, and having

---

[113] Clogy, *Memoir of the life and episcopate of Dr William Bedell*, p. 52. The commission held at least one meeting in Culme's house: Shuckburgh (ed.), *Two biographies of William Bedell*, pp 99, 104; TCD, MS 833, fo. 127r.

[114] TCD, MS 833, fos 78r, 131v.

[115] Ibid., fos 127v, 131r. Mary was the daughter of Sir Faithful Fortescue – she died in 1694: Manning, *Clogh Oughter Castle*, p. 33n.

[116] TCD, MS 833, fo. 127v. For more on the house, see Manning, *Clogh Oughter Castle*, appendix 1.

[117] TCD, MS 833, fo. 114r.

[118] Ibid., fo. 115v.

[119] Ibid., fo. 131r.

gathered up those of his children that he could find, they travelled to Dublin, where he gave his deposition on 9 May.[120]

There was not much sympathy for Culme among some of the settlers, as he had neglected the weapons' store at Clogh Oughter to the extent that although Culme had 'ten pounds worth of sugar and plums, yet he had not one pound of [gun]powder, nor one fixt musquet for the defence of it'.[121] Culme, unsurprisingly, made no mention of this in his own deposition, but it is instructive that it was his kinsman Anthony, and not Arthur himself, who held the key for the castle when the rebels arrived at his door in October 1641.[122] He does seem to have built up good relationships with some of the Gaelic Irish, however, as Culme credited his gaoler, Owen Mac Turlagh Rely, whom Culme noted as being 'a most civill man', as being the 'contynuall preserver of his life', as his life was threatened regularly by other gaolers.[123] Additionally, Philip MacMulmore O'Reilly was present at Culme's house when the rebels arrived, as Jones himself noted in the *Relation*, 'under colour of accustomed friendship', and pleaded for the planter's safety.[124]

It is ironic, given his perceived lack of interest in military matters, that when Culme managed to escape Cavan,[125] he joined the army, rising to a rank higher than his father (who had been a captain), that of lieutenant colonel. Culme also wrote and published in 1647 a diary of events in and around Dublin in early August that year.[126] Arthur died at the siege of Clonmel in May 1650 as part of the Cromwellian army and in his will, he detailed the bequests to be left to his wife Mary, his children Hugh, Elizabeth, Philip, Arthur and Anna, his brother Amedas and his uncle

---

[120] Ibid.

[121] Shuckburgh (ed.), *Two biographies of William Bedell*, p. 190.

[122] Jones was in England when Arthur gave his deposition to the commission in Dublin: TCD, MS 833, fos 127v, 132v. It is perhaps not surprising that no deponents spoke negatively about Culme, given that his brother-in-law was chairing the commission; instead, it took Alexander Clogy, writing years afterwards, to do so: Shuckburgh (ed.), *Two biographies of William Bedell*, p. 190.

[123] TCD, MS 833, fos 127v, 131r.

[124] Ibid., fo. 128r. See below, p. 36.

[125] Alexander Clogy wrote that Arthur was mentioned, along with others who had been held captive at Clogh Oughter, including Bedell's children, in the articles of agreement made between the O'Reillys and Francis Hamilton on 4 June 1642, but, as noted above, this was not the case as Culme was freed in April: Shuckburgh (ed.), *Two biographies of William Bedell*, p. 211; see below, pp 59–62.

[126] Arthur Culme, *A diary and relation of passages in, and about Dublin* (London, 1647). This was published, like Jones' *Relation*, by Godfrey Emerson at the sign of the swan in Little Britain.

Benjamin.[127] His granddaughter Jane (possibly named after Jones' wife) sold the Culme estates in Cavan to the Maxwells of Farnham in 1715.[128]

## Jones' experiences in Cavan as recounted in the *Relation*

As we know, the rising broke out in Ulster over the weekend of 22–23 October 1641. Jones did not leave a particularly detailed deposition relating his experiences in Cavan, although he did make a note of his losses and gave a few lines explaining how he had left Cavan with his family. Instead, he used his statements to push the theory that what was happening in Ireland was part of a larger, papally-sponsored plot designed to rid Europe of Protestantism.[129] So the *Relation* is the best description we have of Jones' experiences in Cavan during the early months of the rising.

On 23 October, Jones recounts, Myles O'Reilly (who reverted to the Gaelic form of his name, Mulmore),[130] who was sheriff of Cavan that year, visited a number of British settlers and fortifications, such as the castle at Farnham, and fooled many settlers into handing over their weapons. He also imprisoned, as we have seen, Arthur Culme, the constable of Clogh Oughter Castle, thus taking into Gaelic hands the most defensible building in the county. Jones went on to describe how the rebels, led by Philip MacHugh O'Reilly and the aforementioned Mulmore, began to take many of the Plantation towns, including Belturbet and Cavan. Much of this Jones would have heard second hand, either on the ground in Cavan, or later as chairman of the deposition commission, otherwise known as the 'Commission for the despoiled subject'. Jones was not impressed by how easily British resistance crumbled in the face of the rising, especially bemoaning what he viewed as the naivety of the settlers in Belturbet, who gave up the town with practically no resistance, despite the warnings form a nearby planter, Sir Francis Hamilton, who cautioned against such an approach. Jones was very complimentary, however, of the two Scottish settlers, Sir James Craig and Sir Francis Hamilton. Between them, as has been discussed, Hamilton and Craig (and following his death, Craig's wife

---

[127] Manning, *Clogh Oughter Castle*, p. 33; NAI, MS T.4861.

[128] Hugh O'Reilly, 'Lisnamaine Castle', *Breifne*, 23 (1985), pp 263–76 at p. 274.

[129] TCD, MS 809, fos 1r–4v; MS 840, fos 32r–v.

[130] Jones was critical of Mulmore, regarding him as someone who betrayed the trust of the British settlers. Jones at one point in the pamphlet referred to O'Reilly in a sarcastic manner as 'the great sheriff', and elsewhere complained about him continuing to use the title of sheriff, which Jones contended he had no right to do. Jones also noted O'Reilly's aloofness, attributing it to the 'state which his assumed greatness had cast upon him'. The fact that Mulmore seized many of Jones' possessions would also have fuelled the dean's antipathy towards him. TCD, MS 840, fo. 32v; see below, pp 45, 56.

and Ambrose Bedell) held out until June 1642, providing a safe haven for many settlers, including acquaintances of Jones', such as Ambrose Bedell, the bishop's son, and Alexander Clogy, the bishop's son-in-law.

At some point in late October or early November 1641, Jones and his family were ejected from their home and taken by the Irish, it seems to the relative safety of Philip MacMulmore O'Reilly's house in Lismore.[131] The rebels had a list of demands which they wanted to send to Dublin, along with somebody who would plead their case. Initially hoping that Bishop Bedell would serve this purpose, he cried off, pleading old age (although he is alleged to have written what was called 'Remonstrance from County of Cavan to Lords Justices and Council at Dublin, 6th November 1641').[132] So the next choice to act as the go-between was Jones himself, who agreed to do so. Jones spent some time in the *Relation* explaining his actions here – the dean may well have felt that he had left himself open to criticism for acting as the rebels' message boy. So Jones in the *Relation* explained his actions, writing that he did the rebels' bidding for two reasons: his safety, and the safety of his family, who remained the captives of the insurgents; and to pass on information to the Dublin government as to the state of affairs in Cavan.[133]

Jones returned to Cavan and his family in Lismore with a vague answer from the Dublin Council to find the county 'all in arms'.[134] Fearing that Dublin was wholly unprepared for an attack upon it by the Gaelic Irish, Jones exaggerated to the O'Reillys the city's strength and preparedness for a military engagement in the hope of delaying or preventing such a move by the Gaelic Irish. Jones attempted unsuccessfully to draw out Mulmore O'Reilly and his plans, but in vain, noting that the sheriff was unforthcoming and 'composed to an unwanted gravity'.[135] Jones had

---

[131] Jones seems to have had a certain amount of freedom to walk around Philip's estate in Lismore and it is implied that he had his own lodging: see below, p. 43. In an apparent attempt to paint all of the Irish insurgents in the same light, Jones excised Philip from the first pamphlet he published in 1642, *A remonstrance of divers remarkeable passages concerning the church and kingdom of Ireland*. But the Gaelic Irishman is portrayed reasonably fairly in the *Relation*: Joseph Cope, 'Fashioning victims: Dr Henry Jones and the plight of Irish Protestants, 1642', *Historical Research*, 74:186 (2001), pp 370–91 at p. 389.

[132] Gilbert Burnet, *The life of William Bedell D.D., lord bishop of Kilmore in Ireland* (London, 1692), p. 184. See below, appendix 3.

[133] It was noted that Jones presented this petition in the company of John Waldron of Farnham. So Jones either travelled to Dublin in the company of Waldron, or else met him in the city prior to submitting the petition to the government there: *Cal. S.P. Ire., 1633–47*, p. 348; TCD, MS 832, fo. 144r.

[134] See below, p. 43.

[135] See below, p. 45.

managed to bribe 'one intimate with' the Gaelic Irish to spy on them and report back to the dean their plans, which he did, the Gaelic Irish being divided in their plans to attack Dublin. Jones got letters to Captain Ryves who had left Belturbet following its fall for Ardbraccan in Meath, alerting him to an Irish plan to attack him and his forces there. Jones also took pain to write in the *Relation* that by staying in Cavan to spy, he was able to alert the privy council in Dublin of the enemy's plans, making his prolonged time among the enemy a profitable one. Jones stayed for a number of more weeks, before he conceived it 'high time to study my coming off'. He is vague about the circumstances of his and his family's escape – 'which by God's assistance was strangely effected' – and so ends Jones' personal involvement with events in Cavan.[136] Everything else that Jones reported from Cavan up until mid-June 1642 came to him second hand. But we do learn that 'with greate hazard of my life & of the lives of my wife & 7 children', he managed to arrive in Dublin, among a group of about forty other English settlers. They were attacked eight times on their journey and robbed of their possessions, but at least managed to arrive in the city relatively unscathed, physically at any rate.[137] On 30 December 1641, headed by Jones and staffed with other Church of Ireland clergymen, work began on the 'Commission for the despoiled subject', which undertook the extraordinary task of taking witness statements from the British refugees.[138]

Jones devoted the remainder of his narrative from his final departure from Cavan, to the experiences of Hamilton and Craig in Cavan, describing skirmishes, the activities of the O'Reillys, the drownings at Belturbet and Hamilton's burning of Killeshandra, the final event which seems to have occurred in early 1642.[139] Jones therefore was not present for these events and was probably told of them by acquaintances or by some of the deponents who gave statements to the commission. The commissioners themselves may have provided some detail in correspondence with Jones when the dean was in London from March 1642. This section of the *Relation* culminates in the sieges of Hamilton's and Craig's castles at Keelagh and Croghan, mentioned above, which began on 4 May 1642 and which forced Hamilton on 4 June to plead for quarter, that, according to Jones, had been offered daily, but up until then had been refused by the Scottish settler.[140]

---

[136] See below, p. 47.

[137] TCD, MS 840, fo. 32v.

[138] The commissioners included William Aldrich, vicar of Drumgoon in the diocese of Kilmore: Aidan Clarke, 'The commission for the despoiled subject, 1641–7' in Brian Mac Cuarta (ed.), *Reshaping Ireland, 1550–1700: colonization and its consequences* (Dublin, 2011), pp 241–60 at pp 243–4.

[139] See below, pp 49–50.

[140] See below, p. 58.

Negotiations began with the Irish and led to the agreement in ten articles which Jones listed in the *Relation*.[141] On 15 June, 1,200 British settlers (800 from Keelagh and 400 from Croghan), along with some supplies and weapons, and joined by a further 140 other British refugees,[142] left in a convoy for Drogheda, described by Alexander Clogy, who was among them, as:

> a sad company of poore people we were, as ever were seene together; some loaden with children, some great with cheild, some two children on their backs, many with two little one in their armes, yet all rejoycing in the Lord for our enlargement at last.[143]

In this trek to safety (it took them the first day to travel the seven miles to Cavan town), they were led by Francis Hamilton to Drogheda and from there to Dublin, where, Jones believed, many intended to take ship to England, 'if they may not be relieved there'.[144] At this point, Jones' narrative ended, the author stating that he intended to take up on a later occasion the story of the entire rising (including Arthur Culme's doomed efforts to recapture Clogh Oughter),[145] something which he never did. Instead, Jones topped and tailed his *Relation* with a letter from his brother-in-law Hugh Culme and the articles agreed upon by the Catholic synod held in Kilkenny in May 1642.[146]

By the spring of 1642, the rising had spread throughout Ireland, but with the insurgents experiencing some setbacks, the need to reorganise was apparent. As the Catholic Church already had an island-wide organisation in place, they took the lead in this reorganisation. Ecclesiastical support for the uprising was formalised at the synod in Kilkenny, carrying on from the one held at Kells in March 1642 under the presidency of David Rothe, bishop of Ossory. The Catholic synod held in Kilkenny on 10, 11 and 13 May 1642 produced twenty-nine articles which Jones published as an addendum to his *Relation* with no comment beyond the detailed description on the cover page.[147] The first name noted in the list of clergy to have attended the synod was 'Hugo Archiepiscopus Armachanus', Hugh O'Reilly, the former Catholic bishop of Kilmore who had been appointed archbishop of Armagh in 1628. He continued to live in the Kilmore area

---

[141] See below, pp 59–62.
[142] As Jones gleefully noted, the settlers managed to take with them more gunpowder than had been agreed: see below, p. 63.
[143] Shuckburgh (ed.), *Two biographies of William Bedell*, p. 212.
[144] Ibid.
[145] No other reference for this appears to exist, even in Culme's own deposition.
[146] See below, appendices 1 and 2.
[147] See frontispiece, p. ii.

of Cavan for at least some years following his elevation to Armagh and it is possible that Jones would have known him personally.[148] The articles which were published from this meeting codified the regulations for the confederacy's future movement and activity, including an oath to be taken by all involved, the return of goods stolen from Catholics which had been recovered 'from the enemy' since October 1641 and the enforcement of law and order throughout Ireland, as well as much more besides.[149] The declaration was made that those who did not take part in the war were automatically excommunicated and that no distinction was to be made between the Gaelic Irish and the Old English communities. Jones, who had gotten his hands on a copy of the articles, made no comment on them, and instead used their content to illustrate the anti-Protestant stance now gaining momentum in Ireland, as well as the losses being endured by the Protestant population in Ireland, most likely in his attempt to secure charitable funding for them.

Having been taking depositions since 3 January 1642,[150] Jones left for London around 9 March 1642 and addressed the House of Commons on the sixteenth of that month, using excerpts from the depositions so far collected to illustrate his presentation. The main thrust of Jones' argument was that the events in Ireland were part of an international conspiracy led by Rome which aimed to wipe out Protestantism. Jones referred to this belief a number of times in his own statements to the commission for the despoiled subject, stating at one point that although 'the firste breaking out of this fire [the rising] into a flame began first on the xxiijth of October 1641 yet was it smoking ... as may well be conjectured, for many yeres before'.[151] The Commons ordered that Jones' address be published and, entitled *A remonstrance of divers remarkeable passages concerning the church and kingdom of Ireland*, it was on sale in London by the end of the month.[152]

Recently described as 'violently anti-Catholic', the *Remonstrance* was designed to emphasise various aspects of the rising and not to chart the

---

[148] Séamus P. Ó Mórdha, 'Hugh O'Reilly (1581?–1653): a reforming primate', *Breifne*, 13 (1970), pp 1–42 at p. 22.

[149] Fearghus Ó Fearghail, 'The Catholic Church in County Kilkenny 1600–1800' in William Nolan and Kevin Whelan (eds), *Kilkenny: history & society* (Dublin, 1990), pp 197–249 at p. 207; Alison Forrestal, *Catholic synods in Ireland, 1600–1690* (Dublin, 1998), pp 103, 123; Patrick J. Corish, 'The rising of 1641 and the confederacy, 1641–5' in T.W. Moody, F.X. Martin and F.J. Byrne (eds), *A new history of Ireland, III: early modern Ireland, 1534–1691* (Oxford, 1987), pp 289–314 at pp 297–8.

[150] Clarke, 'The commission for the despoiled subject, 1641–7', p. 245.

[151] TCD, MS 809, fo. 1r. See also, TCD, MS 840, fos 32r-v.

[152] Clarke, 'The commission for the despoiled subject', p. 247.

course of events as they occurred.[153] For this reason, Jones emphasised the words allegedly uttered by the Irish insurgents, including those who defended their actions by claiming to have had the king's commission directing them in this manner. This, perhaps unsurprisingly, drew a sharp rebuke from Charles I, which led the commission in Ireland to select twenty short quotations from the depositions collected thus far which made clear the traitorous intent of the rebels', a move which seems to have placated the king to some extent.[154] The presumption implicit in the *Remonstrance* was the complete innocence of the British settlers and Protestants attacked since October 1641.[155] Remaining on in London in his attempt to secure aid for those affected by the rising, Jones published, on 11 August, his *Relation*. On the following day, a Commons committee accepted and adopted Jones' recommendations for funding to be allocated in Ireland for the survivors of the rising.[156]

So, why did Jones publish the *Relation*, his account of the rising in Cavan? Financial motivations may have been a consideration – Jones must have been living in extremely straitened circumstances following the events in Cavan. But it also seems, from his remarks in the introduction and conclusion to the pamphlet, that Jones envisaged this to be an initial attempt at relating the overall events of the rising:

> purposing further to enlarge it in many remarkable passages in the general treatise, that shall hereafter (God willing) be set forth, of the whole progress of that war throughout the whole kingdom, as leisure and encouragement shall be thereunto afforded.[157]

The *Relation*, then, was to be the starter aimed at whetting the appetite of the general readership who would have already read Jones' *Remonstrance* and were hungry for more detail from Ireland. Jones also seems to have hoped that by detailing to the Commons the degree to which English law and order had failed in Ireland, he could shock that House into relieving the British settlers affected by the rising, which, as we have seen, they did, the day following the publication of this pamphlet.

---

[153] Patrick Little, 'The politics of preferment: the marquess of Ormond, Archbishop Ussher and the appointment of Irish bishops, 1643–47' in idem (ed.), *Ireland in crisis: war, politics and religion, 1641–50* (Manchester, 2020), pp 138–154 at p. 144.

[154] Clarke, 'The commission for the despoiled subject', pp 248–9.

[155] Cope, 'Fashioning victims', p. 391.

[156] Clarke, 'The commission for the despoiled subject', p. 252.

[157] See below, p. 34.

It may be that Jones had received some criticism for his role in acting as a messenger for the rebels, and had attracted some suspicion relating to his activity while in Cavan, as he took some pains to explain the reasons for his actions at this point. Admitting that some of his motivation was influenced by considerations of his personal safety, Jones also claimed that he accepted the rebels' commission in order to lay 'open to the lords, what I had observed in the proceedings of that county',[158] in other words, to act as a spy for the British authorities. He was at pains to point out that he was forced to return as his family were still imprisoned in Cavan, and that when he spoke with Mulmore O'Reilly, the former sheriff of Cavan, he exaggerated the strength of the Crown forces in Dublin in an attempt to dissuade the rebels from marching on the capital. According to Jones, he managed to turn one of the Irish who had access to the leadership of the Cavan rebels, who kept him informed of their activities. But by early December, Jones, according to himself at least, 'conceived it high time to study my coming off ... which by God's assistance was strangely affected'.[159] This is quite vague, and Jones admitted that his decision to escape was triggered by the return of the Irishman whom he had turned (a former servant) to the Irish camp. Again, this story stretched the credulity of some who heard it, many of whom, Jones acknowledged, 'conceived [it] strange, that in all the time I was not found out by their means'.[160] So Henry Jones' *Relation* was both a further plea to the people of England for charity and a defence of his own actions during the early days of the rising. For a man so obsessed with the apostacy of Protestants in Ireland, it was doubly important that he be above reproach, even if his excuses were threadbare.[161] The income from the pamphlet, as alluded to above, would not have been unwelcome either.

## Later life[162]

At some point between 1641 and 1646, Jones' first wife, Jane Culme, died, although the circumstances and date of her death are unknown to us now. His second marriage, in 1646, was to Mary Piers, the daughter of Sir William Piers in Westmeath. In the first half of the 1640s, Jones remained loyal to Charles I, who was embroiled in the civil war then tearing England apart. He was consecrated bishop of Clogher in 1645 with the support of

---

[158] See below, p. 47.
[159] Ibid.
[160] Ibid.
[161] Cope, 'Fashioning victims', pp 385–7; Annaleigh Margey and Elaine Murphy, '"Backsliders from the Protestant religion": apostasy in the 1641 depositions', *Archivium Hibernicum*, 65 (2012), pp 82–188.
[162] This section is heavily indebted to Aidan Clarke's biography of Jones: *DIB, s.v.*, 'Henry Jones'.

his uncle, James Ussher, and the following year succeeded Ussher as vice-chancellor of Trinity College, Dublin.[163] Henry's brother Michael was made commander of the parliamentary army in Ireland in 1647 and the Jones brothers worked closely together for the next two years until Michael's death from fever.[164] In 1649, Henry was made scoutmaster-general by Oliver Cromwell and was heavily involved in the collection of further depositions in the early 1650s as part of a drive to charge and try those responsible for atrocities against the British in Ireland.

But Jones, as his most recent biographer has noted, fell out of favour with the Protectorate in late 1655 and was instead demoted to the post of official historian on a smaller salary. And following the fall of Richard Cromwell in May 1659, Jones, along with his brother Theophilus, was part of the overthrow of the Protectorate in Ireland. Henry was reckoned in 1660 to be one of a small group in control of the army in Ireland and on 24 May, Jones, who had been promoted to high office under Cromwell, preached the sermon in Christ Church at the thanksgiving service for the restoration of Charles II to the throne. In 1661, Jones was promoted to the bishopric of Meath, a wealthier diocese which also came with a seat on the Irish privy council, recognition of his political nous. It was during his time as bishop of Meath, later in that decade, that Jones donated the Book of Kells and the Book of Durrow to Trinity College, Dublin.[165] He worked on having Bedell's translation of the Old Testament brought into print and wrote of his conviction of the need to evangelise using the Irish tongue. Jones in the late 1670s became involved in Archbishop Oliver Plunkett's trial, gathering information for the accusers and assisting in having the trial moved to London, where Plunkett was tried, found guilty and executed in 1681. Jones himself died shortly thereafter, on 5 January 1682, and was buried in St Andrew's Church in Dublin.

---

[163] Patrick Little, 'Michael Jones and the survival of the Church of Ireland, 1647–9', *Irish Historical Studies*, 163 (2019), pp 12–26 at p. 19. Upon hearing an unfounded rumour of Archbishop Ussher's death, Jones was recommended to the archbishopric of Armagh by the duke of Ormond: Little, 'The politics of preferment', pp 146–7.

[164] Little, 'Michael Jones and the survival of the Church of Ireland, 1647–9', p. 26.

[165] Jones was a significant benefactor of his *alma mater*. A plaque which is now displayed in the Henry Jones Room in the Old Library at Trinity College, Dublin, reads (in Latin): 'Sacred to the memory of Reverend Henry Jones, Doctor of Sacred Theology, Vice-Chancellor of this University, who fitted out and enriched this library at his own expense with a most splendid staircase, windows, shelving, seats and other ornaments in the year 1651'. My thanks to Aisling Lockhart of the Manuscripts Department, Trinity College, Dublin, for her assistance in this matter.

Henry Jones' life was one of peaks and troughs – the rapid rise through the ranks of the Church of Ireland, followed by the losses he experienced in 1641 and afterwards. His important work establishing and heading the 1641 commission, followed by his nomination to the bishopric of Clogher and his promotion to high office in the Protectorate in Ireland, only to fall foul of Cromwell and lose his vaunted position. His final years under the Stuart dynasty brought to Jones the bishopric of Meath and a welcome stability and certainty of purpose. Certainly, historians have much to be thankful to Jones for – as the man who established the Commission for the despoiled subject, he is responsible for the gathering of almost 8,000 witness statements concerning the 1641 rising, a resource unparalleled in early modern European history. He also saved Bedell's translation of the Old Testament and supported its publication, which eventually occurred in 1685, three years after Jones' death. Jones also arranged for the Book of Kells and the Book of Durrow, two national treasures, to be taken into the care of Trinity College, Dublin, where they have been held safely ever since. Henry Jones' *Relation* of the 1641 rising in Cavan, is, in its own way, another Irish treasure, and one which gives the reader further insight into Jones himself and the rising in Cavan, providing us with detail and information which is unavailable elsewhere. The *Relation*'s extra information is what makes this pamphlet such an important, if overlooked, source relating to the early months of the rising. It is hoped that this new edition will address this oversight and add another voice and point of view to the extraordinary corpus of material known today as the 1641 depositions.

## The pamphlet

Henry Jones' pamphlet of the *Relation* was published on 11 August 1642 for Godfrey Emerson, a London printer, and was sold at the 'signe of the Swan in Little-Britain'.[166] The pamphlet comprises two separately numbered sections: one of four pages (including the cover and a blank inside cover page, and two further pages, which are numbered pages 1–4. The main body of text then begins at page one again and runs for forty numbered pages. The separate pagination for the letter, along with its date (4 August), implies that this was a late addition to the pamphlet. The pagination in the main section of the pamphlet is on occasion faulty, since what should be p. 9 is instead p. 17, and runs on from that number for the rest of the pamphlet, only for further issues at what should be pp 42–43 and 46–47 (under this new pagination), but which are actually numbered pp 34–35 and 38–39 respectively. Going by the original pagination, pp 34–35 and 38–39 are actually correct.

---

[166] See frontispiece, p. ii.

The pamphlet itself is split into three sections:

- pp 3–4: a letter from Hugh Culme to Henry Jones, dated 4 August 1642, providing an update of events in the north-east of Ireland in the summer of that year;[167]

- pp 1–40: Jones' account of the rising in Cavan from the outbreak of the rising, including the articles of agreement between Philip McHugh McShane O'Reilly and Francis Hamilton for the surrender of Croghan and Keelagh (pp 36–38) and the safe passage of the British settlers from there on 15 June 1642;

- pp 40–48: The acts passed by the synod held in Kilkenny from 10–13 May 1642.[168]

The same text and printed layout (replete with identical pagination errors) was also published the same day by the same publishers under a slightly different title of *A remonstrance of the beginnings and proceedings of the rebellion in the county of Cavan*.[169] Printing the same book or pamphlet under a different name, even on the same day, was not that unusual, the idea being that it could be sold again to gullible readers.[170] For the sake of completion, appendix 3 below is a transcription of the petition which Jones brought to Dublin and the reply from the Dublin government with which he returned.

---

[167] Appendix 1 below.

[168] Appendix 2 below.

[169] Henry Jones, *A remonstrance of the beginnings and proceedings of the rebellion in the county of Cavan, within the province of Ulster in Ireland, from the 23 of October, 1641, untill the 15 of June, 1642. Whereof hitherto nothing hath been reported. Whereunto is added, the acts, and twenty nine conclusions of that great and generall congregation of archbishops, bishops, and others, all of the Romish clergy in Ireland, met in the city of Kilkenny in that Kingdom, on the 10, 11 and 13 of May 1642. Concerning the present state of the warre in Ireland, and for the ordering of matters appertaining to the same, both there, and by negotiation with forraign princes. Written, set forth, and presented to the most honourable the Houses of Parliament, By Henry Jones, DD. There is also a letter written from Dublin, August 4 1642. Containing some late and very remarkable passages.*

[170] The entire contents of the pamphlet were also published in sections in J.T. Gilbert (ed.), *A contemporary history of affairs in Ireland from 1641 to 1658* (Dublin, 1879), i, part ii, pp 413–19, 476–97, 519–20.

# Henry Jones'
## *Relation*

## The beginning and progress of the rebellion in the county of Cavan, in the province of Ulster in Ireland from October 23 1641, unto June 15 1642

The county of Cavan, whereinto no part of our forces hath hitherto made any the least impression, is at this time the receptacle of all the rebellious lords, gentlemen, and other their adherents, who have been forced out of the counties of Dublin, Meath, Louth, Monaghan, Fermanagh, and elsewhere thereabout, where our armies have, by God's power, victoriously marched. From hence were sent out the first of that rebellious rout, who durst assume the boldness, by leaving their own seats, to make incursions upon us, overrunning the county of Meath, and surprising the towns of Trim, Kelles, Navan, Ardbraccan, Athboy, and thence proceeding to the siege of Drogheda. And from this place, it is feared, they may again show themselves, to our disadvantage, if it be any longer, as it hath been hitherto, neglected. Which, that it may not; I have herein offered a brief discourse of the strength and proceedings of the rebel in that part, from the 23 of October, 1641 until the 15 of June, 1642 purposing further to enlarge it in many remarkable passages in the general treatise, that shall hereafter (God willing) be set forth, of the whole progress of that war throughout the whole kingdom, as leisure and encouragement shall be thereunto afforded.

The 23 of October, 1641 was the day set down by the conspirators, for the general undertaking and practice of that most horrid rebellion; yet did it not, notwithstanding, in all places appear at once; partly out of the backwardness of some, who would first in the proceedings of others, see how far, and with what security they might put themselves upon that work; partly by a forelaid compact[1] that some (they especially of the Irish lords, and others in the counties of Dublin, Meath, Louth, and some other parts of Leinster) pretending to join for the public service against the Ulster rebels, as did their ancestors in the former rebellions, they might procure arms out of the store at Dublin, which they wanted, and which might after be employed against us. This some obtained, though but sparingly; for the lords justices and council finding their own weaknesses for the present conceived it not expedient, by discovering of suspicion, to give them occasion at that time to break out, against whom we might after if they did, be better prepared. Some also were the longer kept off from declaring themselves, by their failing in the first and main act, the surprising of the castle of Dublin; and others being for some while started at the resolution

---

[1] An already agreed plan.

of the honourable houses of parliament in England, for the sending into Ireland great and speedy supplies of men and money.

Yet if any were backward, the Ulster rebels were not; and among them, none more forward the Irish in the county of Cavan consisting of the septs, of the Reilys in chief, and the Mac Gawrans,[2] Bradys, Siridens,[3] Mac Karvans, and Macabes, with others of inferior note. Of these, Philip Mac Hugh Mac Shane O'Reilly was chosen for chief commander, he being head of the sept of the O'Relys and in parliament appearing as knight of the shire for that country.[4]

But he who first appeared as head in this action, was the then high-sheriff of that country, formerly writing himself Miles Reilly, but having with the shaking off of his obedience to the English government, cast off what might in his name sound English, he is now known by the name of Mulmore mac Edmond O'Reily.[5]

This desperate young man first lead the way; and on the Saturday in the afternoon being the 23 of October, 1641 by virtue of his office he raised the *posse comitatus*,[6] pretending that some rebels were either already or ready to break in upon the country from the adjoining counties; his first work was upon this pretence, and for the public service, to gather in what arms were in the hands of the British who dwelt scatteringly, they thereby so wanting the advice and assistance of each other. All this was in that part of the country where he dwelt,[7] done almost in a moment by his bailiffs and agents to that end disposed in all places; he himself going about where he conceived his presence was most requisite to this work; whereby all that part of the country was suddenly disarmed, excepting such places of strength, and persons of note, whom he would not acquaint with this pretence, lest they might find out the feat. All this was done without any show of violence or injury to any, either in word or action; many offering

---

[2] Now known as McGovern.

[3] Sheridans.

[4] This was the formal title for a member of parliament representing a county constituency. Philip was born in 1599, the son of Hugh O'Reilly. He was a soldier who served as a commander of foot and horse in France and was expelled from the House of Commons on 16 November 1641: Bríd McGrath, 'A biographical dictionary of the membership of the Irish House of Commons, 1640–1641' (unpublished PhD thesis, Trinity College, Dublin, 1997), pp 231–2.

[5] Jones pinpoints Myles/Mulmore O'Reilly as the early leader of the rising in Cavan, and not Philip.

[6] The *posse comitatus*, which is Latin for 'power of the county', refers to a group of people mobilised by a sheriff to suppress lawlessness or defend the county.

[7] Myles lived close to Jones in the Ballinagh/Kilmore area.

up their arms,[8] and applauding the care and diligence of the sheriff for the defence of the country, others not yet meddled withal, nothing doubting their own security, while they saw others no way (as they did conceive) damnified.

But this rebel had soon unmasked himself, when within a few hours, the same day, he first entered the castle of Farnam,[9] within one mile of the town of Cavan, and thence took out arms, pikes, and muskets, but none fixed, to many as might arm more than fifty men; and forthwith with his rabble of followers posted to Cloghouter,[10] three miles thence, where, under colour of accustomed friendship he embraced, but there taking prisoner Arthur Culme esquire, captain of his majesty's fort of Cloghouter (a fort of great strength, environed with a deep water, and distant from shore more than musket shot). The captain he laid up in the castle, committing both to the charge of Owen O Rely, with the title of constable of the castle of Cloghouter.

Next day being the 24, this sheriff with what forces he could raise on the sudden in that part of the county, processed to meet with Philip Mac Hugh O Reyly, the chief commander, and with his forces preparing to make their approaches to Belturbet, which, though it were not the county town, yet was it the most populous, and of all others the best English plantation in that county, there being supposed to have been at that time about 1500 of all sorts, of all which 4 or 500 were men for service, were they armed accordingly.

This was by the rebels conceived to be first secured, lest discovering their intent they might make head, and so hinder their proceedings elsewhere; yet could they not come so soon, neither did they carry the matter with a pretext so fair, but that they were found out; for besides the report of taking Captain Culme prisoner, and securing the fort for themselves, which no way sorted

---

[8] This points to a trust which had grown up between settler and native in the thirty or so years since the Plantation. For more on this, see Scott, 'Select document: Petition of the inhabitants of Cavan to the lord deputy and council, 8 July 1629'. Another viewpoint is expressed in Edwards, 'Out of the blue? Provincial unrest in Ireland before 1641'.

[9] Farnham Castle, which lies one mile or so from Clogh Oughter, was planted originally by the Waldron family. Richard Castledine, who was imprisoned on Clogh Oughter as part of Bishop William Bedell's entourage, left his estate at Farnham to his son-in-law John Waldron, and in 1664, to satisfy gambling debts, another of the Waldrons, Sir Thomas, sold the estate and castle to Robert Maxwell, Church of Ireland bishop of Kilmore, thus establishing the Maxwell family in Cavan for over 300 years: TCD, MS 832, fo. 144r; MS 833, fos 115r, 127r; Jonathan Cherry, 'The Maxwell family of Farnham, County Cavan: an introduction', *Breifne*, 42 (2006), pp 125–47 at p. 127.

[10] See above, p. 18.

with what at first they had given out, they were fully discovered by many pillaged and stripped English, who out of the neighbour county of Fermanagh had escaped the fury of that monster of men, Roury mac Guyre,[11] brother of the Lord mac Guyre,[12] and head of the rebels in that county, who had the same time been on the same work that were these in the county of Cavan. To which also was added, that Sir Francis Hamilton, knight and baronet, having received intelligence of these proceedings, had sent unto Belturbet, and Cavan, desiring they would stand upon their guard, and not be deluded with pretences, as were others. After sending particularly unto Captain Robert Bailey, who commanded a Foot company in the town of Cavan, and to Captain Richard Ryves, commanding Sir John Borlase's troop,[13] and garrisoned in Belturbet; that they would draw to him towards Keilay,[14] a place of strength, that joining to them the British about Belturbet, Cavan, and elsewhere, they might in an united body make head against the rebel. Had this course been taken, there might have been made up a body of 1000 men, if perhaps that number would not rather have doubled by the coming into them of such British as fled to the county from Fermanagh in very great multitude. Hereby might the proceedings of that rebel have been at a stop, if not wholly defeated, and they kept in work at home, so as they should not (as they did after) intend the sending of forces to Droghedah, which they could not have spared. But why this did not take, I cannot answer.

If it be not attributed to the sudden confusion of all things, the time admitting no deliberation, and this proposition from Sir Francis Hamilton being words at distance, wanting the presence of such as might give them a

---

[11] Rory Maguire was one of the leaders of the rising in Fermanagh and became a notorious figure among the settlers: Brendan Scott, 'The Maguires and Fermanagh, 1603–1720' in Raymond Gillespie and Brendan Scott (eds), *The Books of Knockninny: manuscripts, culture and society in early eighteenth-century Fermanagh* (Cavan, 2019), pp 11–24 at pp 14–16.

[12] Conor Maguire, the second Lord Enniskillen, was one of the conspirators of the 1641 rising. Captured in Dublin at the outbreak of the rising, he was tried and executed for treason in February 1645: Charlene Adair, 'The trial of Lord Maguire and "print culture"' in Eamon Darcy, Annaleigh Margey and Elaine Murphy (eds), *The 1641 depositions and the Irish rebellion* (London, 2012), pp 169–83, 235–8.

[13] Sir John Borlase was an English army officer who represented Belturbet as an MP in the House of Commons in 1639. He was appointed joint Lord Justice of Ireland alongside Sir William Parsons in February 1641 and served in that position until their dismissal in January 1644: *Oxford DNB, s.v.*, 'Sir John Borlase'.

[14] Keelagh was close to Killeshandra and the site of Sir Francis Hamilton's bawn. See Introduction.

full discussion, and answer the objections that might be brought unto them. Captain Ryves upon the first hearing of these tumults made ready of his troop as many as were not dispersed in the country; for the present making up the number of thirty. Then did he call upon the townsmen of Belturbet to stand upon their defence, which they prepared with all forwardness to do, until that Philip mac Hugh O'Reily and other heads of the rebels had sent to Belturbet, professing themselves ready for their defence against the incursions of Roury mac Guyre in the next county,[15] who threatened (as they gave out) to break in upon them, they promising to put a guard into the town for their security, without the least prejudice to any [of] the inhabitants, either in person or goods. The town also sending out some to treat with the rebels, whom they found to intend more than was pretended; but doubting their own strength for opposition, the place being not defensible, the church being all the guard it had,[16] and hearing the rebels to be about 4000 strong. Hereupon Captain Ryves, conceiving it time for him to provide for his security with those few men he could on the sudden get together, posted towards Cavan, the country and time of the year being not for service of horse,[17] and knowing the aim of the enemy to be chiefly for surprising him and his arms. From Cavan after some little stay, he set forward by Dalys Bridge,[18] and so recovered Ardbraccan, a strong castle of the bishop of Meath's,[19] twenty-two miles from Dublin, where, by command from the lords justices he remained for securing that part of the country. He being thereby reserved for those honourable services which since that time he hath done, in them much deserving of the public.

The treaty between the townsmen of Belturbet and the rebels had now proceeded so far that they put themselves into the protection, and under that guard placed there by Philip O Reyly, having first given up their arms, so as now they rested wholly at their mercy, yet violence for that time not being offered unto any.

Belturbet being thus secured for their own, they did next look towards Cavan, the county town, and seven miles from Belturbet. The place was not

---

[15] Belturbet lies very close to the Fermanagh border.

[16] Belturbet's Church of Ireland church, built in the 1630s, occupied a high vantage point in the town. A star-shaped fort was constructed there in 1689, and it is possible that there was an earlier defence feature on the site as well: Scott, *Belturbet, County Cavan, 1610–1714*, p. 53.

[17] The roads were generally more impassable during the winter, meaning it would be difficult to move large numbers of horse through the countryside.

[18] Daly's Bridge is the former name of what is now known as Mountnugent, County Cavan, which borders the county of Meath. See p. xii.

[19] This was the traditional seat of the bishop of Meath.

defensible, the most part of the inhabitants also being Irish and papists;[20] so that Captain Bayly was enforced to betake himself into the county gaol,[21] the place of greatest strength that was there, yet indeed of no strength of oppose an enemy. His company at the full was but fifty, of which many were then absent, and the most of those that were present were Irish, upon whom he could not rely: besides, that he wanted powder, having no more, or not much more than his Bandeleers to trust unto. The enemy came in with 3000 men, besides a confused multitude of others, followers of the army, against whom the town could make no resistance, and the castle was by them summoned, but all partly rejected by the captain, thereby more to make trial of the revolutions, and to find out the proceedings of the enemy, than out of any confidence he had of any resistance that by him could be made. The same countenance he held that 25 and the following 26 of October, until feeling to be overcome with the importunity of some friends, sent to treat with him, rather than out of any diffidence of his own condition, the parley was entertained the 27 day and the place yielded on composition that the arms of the company should pass away, and be in the captain's custody within his own house, about one mile distant from the Cavan, and that the captain should neither send them, nor join himself with Sir Francis Hamilton at Keilagh, Sir James Craig at Crohan,[22] both not far off, neither with any other British within the country, neither that the arms should be carried out of the county.[23]

On the 29, the sheriff with 3000 men passing by the castle of Belanenagh, where I then lived, and which I did maintain from the 23 until then, did require the surrender of the place, which not being to be maintained, in many respects was yielded, I being with mine committed to

---

[20] The first corporation there, established in 1610, was almost entirely Gaelic in composition: Jonathan Cherry, 'The indigenous and colonial urbanization of Cavan town, *c.* 1300–*c.* 1641' in Scott (ed.), *Culture and society in early modern Breifne/Cavan*, pp 85–105 at pp 93–4. See also the deposition of Stephen Allen, sovereign of Cavan town in 1641, in which he criticises what he sees as the disloyalty of the Irish living in Cavan at the outbreak of the rising: TCD, MS 832, fos 174r–175v.

[21] The gaol was noted in 1614 for its squalid and cramped conditions: Vera Moynes (ed.), *Irish Jesuit annual letters 1604–1674*, 2 vols (Dublin, 2019), i, pp 407–08.

[22] Croghan lay close to Killeshandra and was the location of Sir James Craig's bawn. See above, pp 15–17.

[23] This indented section appears in quotation marks in the pamphlet, so seems to be representing the wording of the agreement made.

the charge of Philip Mac Mulmore O Reily, uncle to the sheriff,[24] living about a mile thence, and a garrison placed in my castle.

Thus the whole county was taken in, within less than a week, excepting the castles of Keilagh, belonging to Sir Francis Hamilton, and of Crohan, where Sir James Craig lived, these being out of the way; being also very strong for defence, well manned, and well stored with arms, the rebels reserved for their better leisure to look after.[25]

Now did the time fully serve to declare themselves; now were all the English whose dwellings were dispersed in the country, and had been hitherto spared, turned out of doors, robbed of all, and stripped naked; now did they fall upon the English at the Cavan, who til then, though living there in fear, [were] yet not expelled. Now began they to look again upon Belturbet, the captains giving way to the garrison to oppress the inhabitants; they complaining of breach of the treaty, were by the chief answered, that it was not in their power to restrain the rude soldier, who would not be under any command, and therefore advised them rather to prepare for their leaving the place, and to retire whither they pleased, which they might (said they) do with all security, taking with them of their own what they pleased, promising them a safe convoy out of the county.

This was by most conceived to be a motion not be refused, for they found the place weary of them, and that to stay, were but to give themselves up to spoil; especially seeing that contrary to the quarter unto them given, their shops were broken up,[26] and the best of their goods already in the hands of their enemies, pretending by making up an inventory of them, and putting them into the custody of responsible men, they might be secured from the rapine and spoil of the rude soldier.

They therefore prepared for their journey, relying (shall I say) on the public faith given unto them by the chief commander, and the rest of the

---

[24] Philip MacMulmore O'Reilly, despite being an uncle to Myles O'Reilly, managed to protect many settlers, including Henry Jones, at his house in Lismore, close to where Crossdoney now lies. A number of depositions note the falling out he seems to have had with his family over the veracity of the king's commission, which, Myles claimed, gave them permission to rise up, but which was in fact a forgery. Philip was imprisoned by the O'Reillys over his stance for a short period in late 1641, but was released soon after: Joseph Cope, 'The experience of survival during the 1641 Irish rebellion', *Historical Journal*, 46:2 (2003), pp 295–316.

[25] Meaning that the Irish would take their time to capture these.

[26] There were at least eight merchants and shopkeepers and sixteen others with trades who possibly had premises (including an innkeeper who was also a tanner), operating in Belturbet prior to the outbreak of the 1641 rising: Scott, *Belturbet, County Cavan, 1610–1714*, p. 15.

captains, whereby many found themselves, as in other respects, so in this deceived, that upon promise they might safely carry away what conveniently they might of the choice of their goods (a policy used by the enemy for possessing themselves of what had been hidden), some did dig up what they had buried, and packed up what was most esteemed of them. Thus did the Lady Butler[27] with her family, and about 1500 souls, men, women and children, set forth together, leaving the town, and putting themselves under the convoy of a number no way considerable for their security.[28]

Their way lay through the town of the Cavan, where was a garrison of the rebels, with whom, in all probability, this their treacherous guard had held correspondence: for (passing by many hard usages of these poor creatures, from their leaving Belturbet til then) as they had a little passed the town of Cavan, they were beset and rifled, their convoy seeming at first to be overborne with number, but they with the rest fell to the same work; whereby some were killed, all stripped, some almost, others altogether naked, not respecting women and sucking infants, the Lady Butler faring herein as did others. Of these miserable creatures many perished by famine and cold travelling naked through frost and snow,[29] the rest recovering Dublin, where now many of them are among others, in the same distress for bread and clothes.

The whole county being now, for the most part, in their own power they spent the time in appointing officers,[30] mustering, and exercising their men; in the mean time consulting how to put a fair gloss (if it were possible) upon all that had been done.

---

[27] Mary Butler (*née* Brinsley) was the English-born widow of Sir Stephen Butler, the undertaker who had planted Belturbet. Following Butler's death in 1638, Mary married one Edward Philpott, who gave a deposition detailing his experiences during the 1641 Rising: Brendan Scott, 'Sir Stephen Butler and other inhabitants of early Plantation Belturbet', *Breifne*, 54 (2019), pp 416–26; TCD, MS 833, fos 182r–v.

[28] The number of displaced settlers in this convoy has been estimated at anything between 1400 and 4,100 people: Scott, *Belturbet, County Cavan, 1610–1714*, pp 21–2.

[29] This period has come to be known as the 'little ice age' due to the inclement weather conditions experienced: Francis Ludlow and Arlene Crampsie, 'Environmental history of Ireland, 1550–1730' in Jane Ohlmeyer (ed.), *The Cambridge history of Ireland, volume II, 1550–1730* (Cambridge, 2018), pp 608–37. See also Scott, *Belturbet, County Cavan, 1610–1714*, pp 20–21.

[30] In Belturbet, the Gaelic Irish retained (at least for a time) the corporation system which had been established by the settlers, and appointed one Owen Brady the new provost: Scott, *Belturbet, County Cavan, 1610–1714*, p. 21.

To this purpose an humble remembrance (for so were they pleased to entitle it) was drawn up, setting forth the grievances of that county, and of the whole kingdom, the pretended causes of their rising up in arms; desiring the lords justices and council (unto whom it was to be presented) that from their lordships they might be recommended to his majesty. That satisfaction to those their desires being given, they promised reparation to all the despoiled British, by a general contribution over the kingdom, if their own estates sufficed not thereunto; professing much detestation of the cruelties and robberies exercised by the rude multitude, whom (said they) they could not rule. All which was subscribed by Philip mac Hugh their general, with others their prime commanders, and gentry of that county.

Their next consideration was whom they should employ in that service; for none of their own had confidence sufficient to appear in that cause. They had first fixed upon Doctor Bedell, bishop of Kilmore; but he fairly excused himself, first by his age,[31] whereby he was unwieldy, and not fit for that expedition which they expected in that action; then, that many of the poor English of Belturbet, who had retired to him, and depended upon what security and subsistence he could give them, would by his absence be exposed to want and other injuries. This they interpreted as a put off; yet did the gravity and respect which his presence did command, restrain them from what some in their council had before propounded, in case he should give out, and decline that service for them. I was next in their eye being in their hands, and designed and commanded upon this implement. I must confess, it was such as was in every respect improper for me to undergo; but weighting first what a denial might produce, by what was threatened to another, whereof he hath since found the effects. But chiefly considering, that thereby I might gain the opportunity of laying open to the lords, what I had observed in the proceedings of that county, which might very much conduce to the public, and which by letters could not to safely be delivered; I did therefore accept of that employment, and after ten days' stay in Dublin, returned with an answer. Return I must, my wife and children remaining for hostages. The answer was fair; but general and dilatory, suitable to the weak condition of affairs in Dublin, the safety whereof wholly depending on the gain of time.

I do assure myself these remonstrants did not expect any other answer; and it may be would have been very unwilling to receive that satisfaction they did pretend to be contented withal; their hopes already soaring at an higher pitch: and very probable it is that their said remonstrance tended rather to win upon the people, whose cause they pleaded, and than to give any reasonable accompt or satisfaction to the lords, concerning their

---

[31] Bedell was almost seventy years old in late 1641: *Oxford DNB*, *s.v.*, 'William Bedell'.

proceedings. If hereunto this be not also added, that all this was but to lull all them in Dublin in security, with a treaty of peace, while they intending nothing less, were even then preparing for war, and ready to set forward for Dublin, where they had overtaken me, had I stayed but ten days more, as may appear by the sequel.[32]

For no sooner was I returned into the county of Cavan, but that I found all in arms, and proclamation to have been made, that all from the age of sixteen to sixty should appear on Monday after at Virginia, a place distant from Cavan twelve miles,[33] and in the way to Dublin. It being already highway news, that out of that multitude, they purposed to frame the body of an army of about 3000, who joining with proportionable numbers out of the counties of Fermanagh and Monaghan, were to advance forthwith towards Dublin.

Being also alighted at the house of Philip mac Mulmore O Reyly,[34] whereunto I had been confined, I found one every way appointed as a trooper, calling himself by the name of Dowdall, but being a friar; who came thither from Dublin, and was sent (as he alleged) from thence to hasten their marching away, assuring them of a strong party in that city; besides those in that garrison (for so it was rather to be seemed than an army) for defence of Dublin; wherein were many of the Irish listed, and such as would revolt unto them with with[35] their arms.

I saw how contrary this their proceeding was to that profession of theirs in their remonstrance, and the promise made to me upon the undertaking that service for them, assuring me, and desiring I should assure the lords from them, that there should be a cessation of all things, until the return of their lordships' answer. I found how dangerous in these respects, this sudden undertaking might be to the lords, who might be surprised, fearing no such danger from those parts among all others. I knew by what I had observed, how unprovided both for men and victuals Dublin was at that time, whereby should the enemy advance according to his design, all might have run an apparent hazard. And that which added to all this, that neither had I any sure hand by whom to send, neither could I give any timely notice of these councils, my coming into the county being on Saturday in the afternoon, and they setting forward on the Monday morning next following. And lastly, that in all this, I wanted a second with whom to advise hereupon.

But taking Horse, I posted to Cavet a place within one mile of me, where dwelt the sheriff, one of the chiefest rebels, at whose house, at that very

---
[32] By what follows.
[33] Virginia is almost seventeen miles from Cavan town.
[34] Philip lived in Lismore, close to Crossdoney, and near to Jones' own house.
[35] A second 'with' was mistakenly added here.

instant, their grand council was met. That which I propounded to myself, was to endeavour all the means I could for diverting them from Dublin, by putting them on upon some other service more easy, and of little less consequence. That also time might be gained by either delaying them some while in the county, while I pretended the giving in an accompt[36] of my agency at a general meeting of the gentleman, when and where I should be appointed, or otherwise by finding them work some other way, without marching outright towards Dublin.

Having alighted at the sheriff's door, he took me aside into his garden, from whom I soon understood how little respect would be given to the answer I was to deliver: no part whereof I would impart to him until I were publicly called upon to declare myself, only for the general, that it was as good as he could expect from the lords in Ireland.

Therefore declining that, I laboured first to make my return unto them a ground of that confidence they might repose in me. That for their advantage, I had observed the condition of affairs, in and about Dublin, which compared with what I found to be now in hand in that county, (for then it was no secret), I thought it my part to offer one and the other to him, that he might order his course in a way most for his security. That besides the great supplies concluded in the parliament of England to be sent into Ireland, which were daily expected, the castle of Dublin was provided of a garrison of 300 men and victualled for six months. That in Dublin the forces were greater than I could believe they could have been; so as if by their late humble remonstrance they had not prevented it, there had before then a strong power been sent against them, which I desired the lords might be kept back until a return, of what effects their answer might produce, were given in unto them. That it was far from all policy for them to engage their first setting forth upon that which would be of greatest opposition. That to receive the least show of a defeat in the beginning of their work, were at once to dishearten their own men, and to keep of others that would according to their success declare themselves for, or against them. That it might be conceived, that the attempting first of Droghedah, though less honourable, compared with the other, yet could be the easier, and every way conducing[37] to the intent of their proceedings. That as that place was strong so was it with little or no difficulty to be taken in, considering the party they had there, and the weakness of the garrison, being none other

---

[36] An account.
[37] Conducing, meaning conducive.

than the Lord Moore's troop.[38] That by attaining that place, as it would be an heartening to his men, so would it open the way for the northern forces to come up and join in any attempt upon Dublin, whereas now it did lie as a stop in their way. That therein they had a place for a safe retreat on any occasion; whereof they could not readily be dispossessed. That whether he attempted the one, or the other of those two places, it were wisdom to spend and spin out some part of the time about Kells, or other parts in Meath, until the other forces of Fermanagh and Monaghan came up unto him. Least by advancing too far upon his own strength, he might be encountered apart by the power of Dublin; and so by too much forwardness endanger the whole. This last was added that thereby, either by letters from me, or by the appearing of the enemy, and not marching forward, notice might be given at Dublin of their proceedings.

I could not conclude of anything I had gained upon him in all this discourse, either by his gesture or words, his countenance was composed to an unwanted gravity; keeping I suppose, the distance, and that state which his assumed greatness had cast upon him. And although I take much, that he deigned me no answer to any part hereof, but drew me off to another matter, and soon after parted from me, yet with respects.

There was one intimate with them, and whom upon promise of pardon and great rewards, I had more than half moulded before to my purpose, and whom I found in many particulars before, to cooperate with me, by keeping in with them to give me intelligence of their designs. Having brought him along with me thither, I left him there to be present in their council, and thereof to give me an accompt[39] with all secrecy and speed, I retiring to my lodging whence I came.

By the return which was made unto me about three hours after (and then it began to be late), I found that they had been divided in their opinions. Some were for a direct marching to Dublin, and giving the onset upon the place, grounding upon the information given them by the friar. Others, doubting what a repulse might produce, conceived it the safest and best course to quarter about Dublin, at some distance, thereby to hinder the going in of provision; to expect a convenient time of assaulting it, if it were found fit to attempt it; to gather all that would join with them thereabouts, whereby they would soon grow to a considerable body for any enterprise and that in the meantime they might divert the water that from

---

[38] Charles Moore, 2nd Viscount of Drogheda. From Mellifont, Moore was one of those who helped to lift the siege of Drogheda in March 1642. He died at the Battle of Portlester on 7 August 1643, killed by a cannonball fired allegedly by Eoghan Roe O'Neill: *Oxford DNB, s.v.*, 'Charles Moore'.

[39] An account.

Templeoge[40] did furnish one part of the city, by which also the mills were kept on work. Either of these might have proved most perilous, but the third was wholly for Drogheda, for the reasons aforesaid, which seemed to weigh down the other two (it may be) because the sheriff was the propounder, and inclined thereunto, yet was it not resolved, until their meeting at Kells, whether of these to fix upon, to which time and place it was deferred.

Thereupon I made ready my letters, and dealt with mine intelligencer for the delivery of them into whose hands I must therein put mine own and the lives of mine. He must have been of necessity on Monday morning at the general meeting at Virginia, whence should he have absented himself, besides what was threatened to any that made default, both of us might have been drawn into suspicion; and by his presence among them, I might further understand of their courses. I obtained therefore this much of him, that he would deliver my letter to a gentleman dwelling within nine miles, or thereabouts, from Arbraccan, whom, in my letter to him, I desired to desired to[41] deliver the enclosed with speed to Captain Ryves, at Arbraccan, which he did, but not with that speed that I desired, and which the cause required, but I thought it not safe to acquaint them with the occasion. In my letter to Captain Ryves, I declared a design the enemy had upon him, purposing to be with him the Wednesday following, and by a drove of cattle that should pass by him, to draw him out of his strength, of which I gave him notice, leaving the rest to himself, desiring that with all speed the enclosed to the lords justices should be dispatched upon sight, being of the greatest concernment. These letters being perused by the lords, they sent their commands to Captain Ryves to retire, which he did, therein preventing the enemy, who the night following took up his quarters. I did also certify their lordships of the whole conceits of the enemies, leaving to their wisdoms to provide both for Drogheda and Dublin; for as they were easily drawn off from Dublin, to think of Drogheda, so might they as readily, alter that resolution again. Wherein their lordships were not wanting; for while the enemy by spending time about Kells, Trim, Athboy, Navan, we gained the opportunity of ordering matters to the best advantage, both for Dublin and Drogheda, yet so as by some miscarriage (I cannot yet say by whose), the enemy met with 600 of our men, sent for a further supply to Drogheda, whom they defeated, and after much mischief thereabouts, settled themselves to the siege of that town; where, by the wisdom and valour of the governor, that place had found them work, to the preservation (in all probability) of Dublin, and therein, of the whole kingdom.

---

[40] Templeogue, a suburb in the south-west of Dublin.
[41] 'desired to' is repeated mistakenly.

As for mine own particular, having many weeks after continued in the house of my bondage, I conceived it high time to study my coming off, by all means; which by God's assistance was strangely effected: till then, my stay was not altogether against my will, while I found myself enabled by intelligence to promote the service of my country. But finding him who was my chief agent, from a neuter, to fall wholly to them; that also some of mine own servants employed by me, was with the enemy at Drogheda; and that the gentleman, the deliverer of that my letter to Captain Ryves at Arbracan, was fallen away, I could not expect, in my stay here, to do any more good, but thereby might rather prejudice myself in the higher degree, were I discovered. And it was by many conceived strange, that in all that time I was not found out by their means. But as I do in the first place make the work to be God's, so do I next attribute it to the having their hands in the work with me, so as they could not but suffer with me.

Hitherto hath been declared the state of matters in that county, from the 23 of October, unto the 11 of December: all being reduced into the hands of the rebels, excepting the two castles of Kylagh and Crohan, maintained against them by Sir Francis Hamilton, knight and baronet, and Sir James Craig, knight.

These two noble knights, upon the first noise of the rebellion, did both awaken the security of others about them, and provided for their own defence. Their castles were strong and defensible, which they furnished with men and victuals. Sir Francis Hamilton had armed two hundred and fifty foot, and thirty-six horse, most of his own tenants: he was stored with three barrels of powder, and laid in provision for six months, which yet fell short of that time, by receiving into his castle of about seven hundred other unserviceable persons, men, women and children almost stripped naked, and flying thither from the fury of the rebels. In Sir James Craig's castle at Crohan, there were one hundred and twenty, besides unserviceable persons, who in like manner were fled thither for refuge, to a great number.

I have before set forth the honourable quarter given unto Captain Bailey, upon the surrender of (what he could not keep) his weak hold at the Cavan, it being conditioned that he should have in his own keeping the arms for his company of 50 men with which they suffered him to pass, and accordingly he passed them without molestation. But it being considered that he was limited to a place of laying them up, and that only in his own house, being covered with thatch, and so easily commanded at their pleasure; he also wanting men for guarding of them, for most of his company were revolted, we have reason to conceive that all this in them was rather a not yet breaking, rather than a keeping of quarter; that under a show of fair dealing, they might draw others who held out, with greater confidence to put themselves into their hands.

This was apparent in their preparation made for their marching towards Drogheda; at which time they concluded the taking into their hands those arms, which at their pleasure they might easily do, and which till then they had forborne to do.

Hereof Sir Francis Hamilton receiving advertisement, the night before this should have been put in execution, he sent out 30 horse, and 20 foot, under the leading of M[r]. Malcolm Hamilton, M[r]. David Creighton[42] and James Somerville, (gentlemen approved for many services then, and after) at the bridge of Ballihillian[43] (called the Black Bridge) they left their foot to make good their retreat, the horse passing forward to the captain's house, whom having mounted, they brought him away together with his ensign, sergeant, colours, and what of the arms they could possibly carry with them; a service as considerable, as it was to the undertakers dangerous. For had the alarm, being given time enough to the enemies being 3000, and lying within less than two miles, and the passage of the Black Bridge taken from them, they could not have escaped; and a miracle it was almost, that in the riding of 6 miles (scarce any by place wanting an Irish cottage) yet they should to pass undiscovered, until they were out of all danger, the enemy afterwards hotly pursuing, but in vain. Some pikes the enemy had after found in the captain's house, which could not in haste by our men be either carried away, or made unserviceable; and some pieces of armour were taken up here and there scattered in the way, being fallen from them; so that now the rebels condemned the keeping of that quarter so long, and that they had before secured that passage, as since that time they did, both by cutting the bridge, being of wood, and placing there a strong guard besides.

This and other incursions out of these two castles made upon the rebels remaining in that country, while their fellows were at the siege of Drogheda, occasioned the sending back from the siege, Edmund O Reyly, father to the sheriff, with command with what forces he could raise, to take in these places; that so they might without any distraction intend their great design abroad.

For affecting hereof, to those raised in that county were joined, others called in from the neighbour country of Letrim, both making up above 2000, whom Edmund their commander conceived more than suspicion for that service, purposing to besiege both castles at once, which he might

---

[42] David Creighton held the manor of Aghalane in the barony of Knockninny, County Fermanagh, which lies very close to the Cavan border. He died without issue in 1644/45: TCD, MS 835, fos 147r, 170r; William Roulston, 'Landed society in Knockninny, *c.* 1660–*c.* 1740' in Gillespie and Scott (eds), *The Books of Knockninny*, pp 25–56 at p. 28.

[43] Ballyheelan is a townland in the civil parish of Ballymachugh.

easily and conveniently have done. For they were within little more than a mile of each other, being on the one side shut in with water over, which at that time there could be for the besieged, no passage; other parts being compassed with woods, fit for the enemy's purpose, wherein they might so have placed themselves, as there could be no getting off that way. In the middle between both castles, did stand the town of Killishandra,[44] belonging to Sir Francis Hamilton, convenient for the enemy's quarters, answering to both places, and suspicion with all conveniency of good houses to lodge the whole army; so that there wanted nothing to advantage the besieges,[45] or to distress the besieged.

Upon intelligence received of their approaching (for the scouts were the only intelligencers) Sir Francis Hamilton sent out a party of Horse and Foot, burning all places about, beginning with his own town of Killishandra, by himself built and planted, that it might not stand the enemy in steed; so also did Sir James Craig, about him; whereby the rebel was disappointed of his quarters; without which he could not subsist in that cold season of frost and snow; finding it more than he was well able to do, to stay there only two nights.

That time of his being there was spent in drawing up towards Sir James Craig's castle of Crohan; whence they were beaten back with their loss of fourteen men, and the taking prisoners of Laughlin O Rourke, and Brian O Rourke, eminent persons among them, and prime leaders of the Leitrim rebels, these were after exchanged by Sir James Craig for Dr Bedell, bishop of Kilmore and some others yet contrary to this agreement did they again lay hold on that reverend person, only affording him a being, where they might at their pleasure command him, where he after died: being one of the brightest lights of that Church, both for learning and a shining conversation, and in his constant diligence in the work of the ministry a pattern to others.

The enemy soon weary of his bad lodging, and worse entertainment, though his loss were not great, his offers of fair quarter being rejected, prepared to be gone: yet not without doing something answerable to the greatness of his preparations and the expectation everywhere had of them: which was the stealing away of some few straggling cattle about the castles. I say stealing them away for he durst not advance within sight or command of musket shot of either, and with those greasy spoils did he return in triumph, supplying what he wanted of doing, with menaces and promises of what he would do.

About a fortnight after, it being given out that they meant to return, Sir Francis Hamilton sent abroad twelve horses to burn all within three or four

---

[44] See above, pp 13–14.
[45] Besieger.

miles about him. In doing whereof, they discovered the enemy drawing towards them, being about three hundred, of which having sent speedy notice to Sir Francis (which also he commanded they should do) who to answer any such occasion, had in readiness other twelve horses and sixty foot, with whom he marched, easily directing his course by the fires his men before sent forth had made, for they according to their directions so avoided the enemy, that yet they still kept them in play, coasting from place to place near about, and firing what they came near, expecting the coming up of their seconds. Sir Francis had in a convenient place for his own restraint, and for distressing the enemy should they follow him, laid forty-five of his foot: and with fifteen of the ablest of them drew up, with whom and his twenty-four horses, he set upon the rebels, at the first volley killing six of them, of whom Fr O Rourke, a friar, was one, who in the habit of his Order did lead the company. At the next there fell nine, the enemy standing to it while most of our bandoleers were spent, but being broken by the horse they fled and were pursued about two miles: thirty-seven of them were slain, the coming on of the night, and the disadvantage of the ways for horse, in respect of their Foot, saving the rest. There were taken prisoners, Owen O Rourke their commander, one of great esteem; and Philip O Reyly, uncle to Philip Mac Hugh O Reyly, colonel (as they call him) of that whole country.

All means were used by treaties, and threatening, for getting off these prisoners; concerning whom Sir Francis was solicited by frequent letters from Edmund O Reyly, but in vain: these being reserved (aspersions of the best respects) to answer any the like occasion that might befall the best of ours.

In such services stood matters in those parts, until the first of February, at which time there was great expectation of what should be done against these two castles by Mulmore O Reyly the sheriff; for so I must still call him, he calling himself so, notwithstanding he had been already discharged, but chiefly to distinguish him from others of the same name, and of less note, he being in their esteem the second in that country.

As the several losses the country received from these few British had before drawn Edmund O Rely with some of his men from before Drogheda, to their proceeding in the same course notwithstanding, and principally the said Edmund's late repulse, with all those forces, and the taking and keeping of their late prisoners, called home from that siege Mulmore O Reyly, for doing what his father Edmund could not.

Wherein we may find of what consequence these seeming slight services have been to hinder the proceedings of the enemy abroad for besides the reserving a considerable number at the first at home so as they could not go forth with their full power, it did daily diminish their army before Drogheda. First, in the coming away of Edmund, then of this Mulmore O Reyly, who though they returned without any great numbers, yet some they had; and those under their command left behind soon after followed them notwithstanding any command to the contrary, weighing the greatnesses of the service in the country of Cavan, by the eminency of the persons sent about it. And judging their labour better spent in maintaining at home what was their own, than losing that and themselves in looking after that they never had and never were likely to have: so that of 3000 men that went out of that country to the siege of Drogheda there remained not 700 with Philip mac Hugh o Rely their chief commander. And the most desperate attempts that have been made either against that town, or for hindering the supplies sent to it by sea, were done by those of this country. Hereby also might appear, could any forces at that time have been spared about Dublin and sent in this country what service they might have done for raising the siege of Drogheda; for the town was blocked up on that part that lay towards Dublin if not only yet chiefly by the Cavan forces, whom we see drawn home by a handful of men. Hereby lastly we may see of what consequence it had been to have since the siege of Drogheda, sent some forces into that part for relieving these two castles, whereby the enemy might still have been kept on work, other places in the same country furnished with the like garrisons, and by burning the rest, not suffering it to be (as now it is) the harbour of those, who, if not prevented, may make the later end with us worse than the beginning.

But leaving this necessary digression, for which I do intend the whole discourse, I return where I left.

Mulmore O Reyly being returned from before Drogheda, where he left Philip mac Hugh O Reyly, he began to gather up his men not doubting to make but one, and that no long work of what he came about. Therein also ambitious of the glory of doing that wherein others had failed. Of such as came along with him, that followed after him, that he found in the country, and whom he called in out of the country of Leitrim, he framed the body of an army of 2700. And that it might not be short in number of that with which he hoped at his first setting out to take Dublin itself, he sent for Robert Nugent of Carleuston in the country of Westmeath,[46] a gentleman of £1500 per annum, who upon promise of the arms in both castles (the question not being of taking the places, but for dividing the spoils) came in person with 300 choice men.

With this army of 3000 men, besides a multitude of others who followed to behold the sport (for no otherwise did they conceive of it) Mulmore did quarter about five miles over night in the places the castles which had not been burnt, purposing to begin the next day & with the day to take all before him.

---

[46] Robert Nugent, from Carlanstown in Westmeath, was noted to have been ejected from his house there 'with tears in his eyes': TCD, MS 817, fo. 23r.

The news hereof did no way dismay those who were to receive them, they being so far from immuring[47] themselves up in their forts, there to expect them, that Sir Francis Hamilton drew up his small number into the field, placing in the lane being the highway leading from Killeshandra to his castle of Kylagh 150 men, some few musketeers[48] being here and there left in places of greatest advantage. And that the enemy might not by making a nearer way to this castle (which he might do) find him work in many places at once, he commanded thirty horse to guard the Windmill-Hill joining to the highway towards Killeshandra by which the enemy must march, being also so near to his castle, that they might hear and understand one another speaking aloud. Behind the horse, he cast up a small sconce of earth guarded with sixteen musketeers, to whom the horse might retire, and both of them to make good that passage. It was also so ordered, that those scattered musketeers that were furthest off having given fire and done their parts there, should retire to the next, and they united doing their duty, to fall together back to the next, doing in like manner, until being forced to give ground they might make a fair and orderly retreat for defence of the castle. The enemy now in sight, put forth some horse to skirmish with ours on the Windmill-hill. Of theirs three fell, and the rest fell off, until by the coming on of the whole body, our horse fell back under the command of the musketeers; who giving fire, the enemy was forced to keep himself to the high-way leading to Killeshandra, making in the street a stand to consider of his course.

His intent was not now, as theirs before, to besiege. The dull proceedings of his father suited not with the ways of this heady young man:[49] he is wholly for the assault. Neither will he begin with Crohan as did the other, but resolved to fall upon that which of the two was the strongest and the best provided place and to keep his first man, Sir Francis Hamilton by whom he was most injured.[50] For at that instant one of the musketeers placed in the lane took aim, and, though at very great distance, knocked down among the company one Fitz-Simonds an ensign-bearer, at whose fall there was a great cry.

Whereupon a hundred commanded musketeers of the enemy fell in within the ditches on both sides the lane, to beat upon ours within the lane, while their main body came directly forward. Both one and the other of

---

[47] To enclose or lock up.
[48] A musketeer was a soldier equipped with a musket, an early type of long gun or rifle. See Hunter and Johnston (eds), 'Men and arms', p. x.
[49] Mulmore's father was Edmund O'Reilly.
[50] Jones means that Hamilton caused the O'Reillys the most trouble during the early months of the rising. Mulmore was also angered by the death of Fitz-Simonds.

Figure 1: Henry Jones, artist unattributed, oil on canvas: collection of Trinity College Dublin. Image courtesy of and reproduced by permission of the Board of Trinity College Dublin, the University of Dublin

Figure 2: William Bedell's tombstone, Kilmore cathedral churchyard.
Courtesy of William Roulston

Figure 3: Old cathedral and bishop's palace, Kilmore. Courtesy of William Roulston

Firstly: That there respects to his Ma[jesty] shall be still reserved, but his government and revenues reduced to some bounds; the rule of y[e] Kingdom to be as after is declared; his ma[jesty's] rents to be brought to the ancient reservations before the plantation; and y[e] customs brought to such a certainty as to them shall be thought fitting.

Secondly: The government of y[e] Kingdom to be in y[e] hands of two L[or]d Justices, one of them being of y[e] ancient Irish race, y[e] other of y[e] ancient British inhabiting y[e] Kingdom.

Thirdly: That a parliament be forthwith called consisting of whom they shall think fitt to be admitted, wherein there own Religious men shall be assistants.

Fourthly: Poynings Act to be repealed, and Ireland declared a Kingdom independent on England, without any reference to it in any case whatsoever.

Fiftly: All Acts prejudicial to the Romish Religion to be taken away. And it to be ensured that there shall be no other profession in y[e] Kingdom but y[e] Romish, the contrary professors to be expelled.

Sixtly: That only y[e] ancient Nobility of y[e] Kingdom should stand, and of them, as shall refuse to conforme to y[e] Romish Religion shall be removed & others put in there roomes. But particularly without any such considerations, y[e] Earle of Kildare to be put by, & one Morice Fitz Thomas of y[e] same house & a consort, put in his place.

Seventhly: All Plantation Lands to be recalled; & y[e] ancient proprietors to be reinvested in there former estates, w[i]th the limitations in there covenants expressed, if they have not sold there interests therein before on valuable considerations.

Eightly: That y[e] respective Counties of y[e] Kingdom be subdivided; & certaine bounds or Baronies to be given into y[e] hands of private gent[lemen] and others of y[e] Nobility dwelling in them who are to be answerable for y[e] government thereof. And for the keeping of a standing army in y[e] Kingdom & the fortifying of all places therein. The Respective Governors of these divisions are to build in y[e] most convenient places fortifications; & to be ready on all risings out of such a number of men well appointed as shall be sett downe for them; & that these governors be of absolute power in there owne precincts only responsible — to y[e] parliam[en]t.

Lastly, for maintaining a correspondencie w[i]th other Nations, & for securing y[e] coasts, & also they may be rend[e]red formidable to others, A Navy of certaine number of ships is to be maintained. That to this end five houses be appointed, one in each province accompting — Meath for one, w[i]th an annual pension of some thousands of pounds to be made up of Lands appropriate to Abbeys, & of a further contribution raised in y[e] respective provinces. That these houses are to be assigned to a certaine order of knights answerable to them of Malta who are to be seamen & to maintaine this fleete. That all prizes a certaine proportion to be laid up in y[e] common banke for y[e] further maintenance of y[e] said fleete, y[e] rest to be divided. That for this purpose y[e] felling of woods serviceable for that use to be forbidden. And y[e] house to this end for the province of Leinster should be Kilmainam, or Howth, y[e] Lord of Howth being otherwise accommodated; y[e] place being esteemed very convenient in respect of y[e] situation.

These are their projects for y[e] future; w[hi]ch as they are vaine, so let god disappoint them of...

As for my private sufferings by this Rebellions route y[e] have lost

| | | |
|---|---|---|
| in cowes, sheepe, swine, riding horses & my studd of mares & colts | 500—0—0 |
| in corne and hay and turffe | 100—0—0 |
| in plate household goodes & bookes | 1200—0—0 |
| in debts by rents in arreare & now due | 483—10—0 |
| | 736—0—0 |
| | 3019—10—0 |

Much piece seized upon by Mulmore m[a]c Edmond Rely of Cavett then shirive of y[e] County of Cavan who with many horse foote tooke possession of my house at Ballanenagh in y[e] said County on Friday y[e] 29. of October 1641. some of my cattell were driven away by some Rebells out of Longford & Leitrim, & y[e] some of them by those of y[e] County, whose names I know not, my servants not being there who might give me notice of them. y[e] rest of my goodes w[hi]ch I had conveyed into y[e] house of Philip m[a]c Mulmore o Rely at Lismore in y[e] County of Cavan I was enforced to leave there... with those I fly away to save my life; it greatly hazard of my life, & of y[e] lives of my wife & children. y[t] I recover Dublin coming on foote, being & several times assaulted... all of us stript some in company to y[e] skin... I was also y[e] lost many writings, evidences y[e] most esteemed of besides what I could not carry with me out of y[e] County of Cavan. Some writings concerning y[e] B[isho]p of Kilaloe & y[e] Sea I were taken from me by way by Richard Darcy dwelling neere Kilmanam in y[e] County of ... who with his company of 100 rebels tooke away what wearing clothes & other things necessary I could conveniently carry along with me.

Hen: Jones

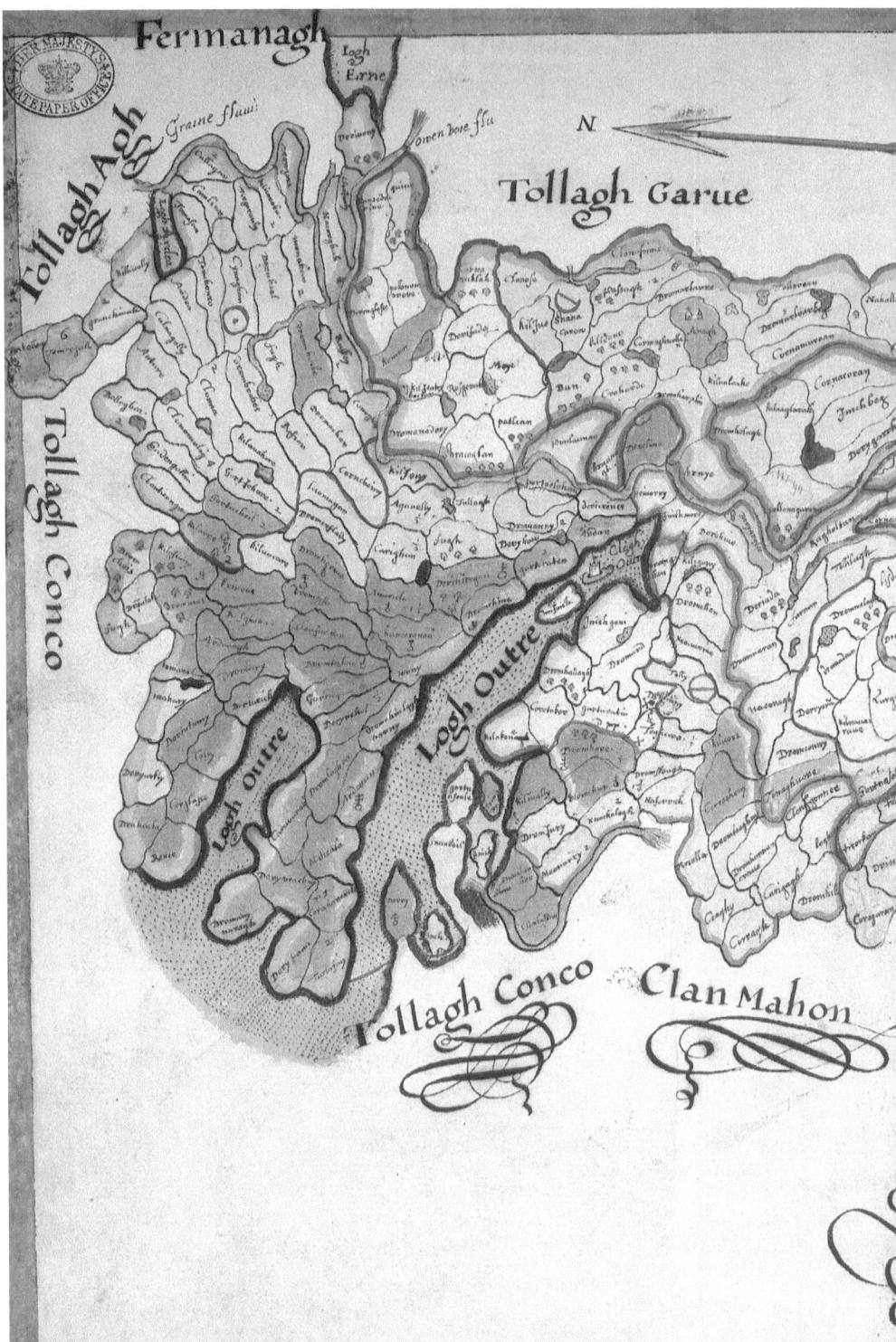

Figure 5: Barony of Loughtee, 1609: TNA, MPF 1/52. Courtesy of The National Archives

## The Baronie of Loghtie

### Tollagh Garue

### Sleugorie Mount

The rest of this greate
Proportion is in
Castle Rahin

### Castle Rahin

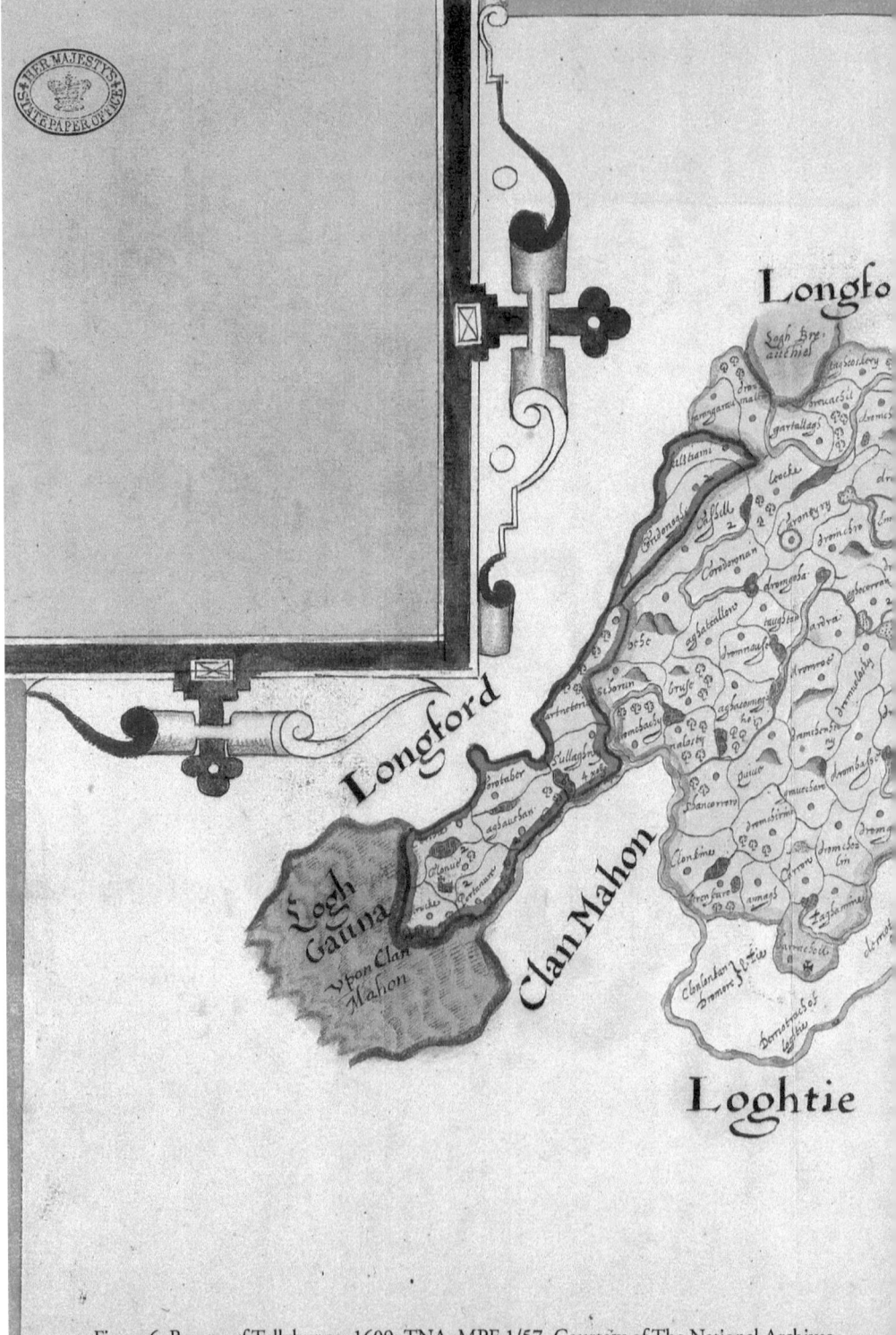

Figure 6: Barony of Tullyhunco, 1609: TNA, MPF 1/57. Courtesy of The National Archives

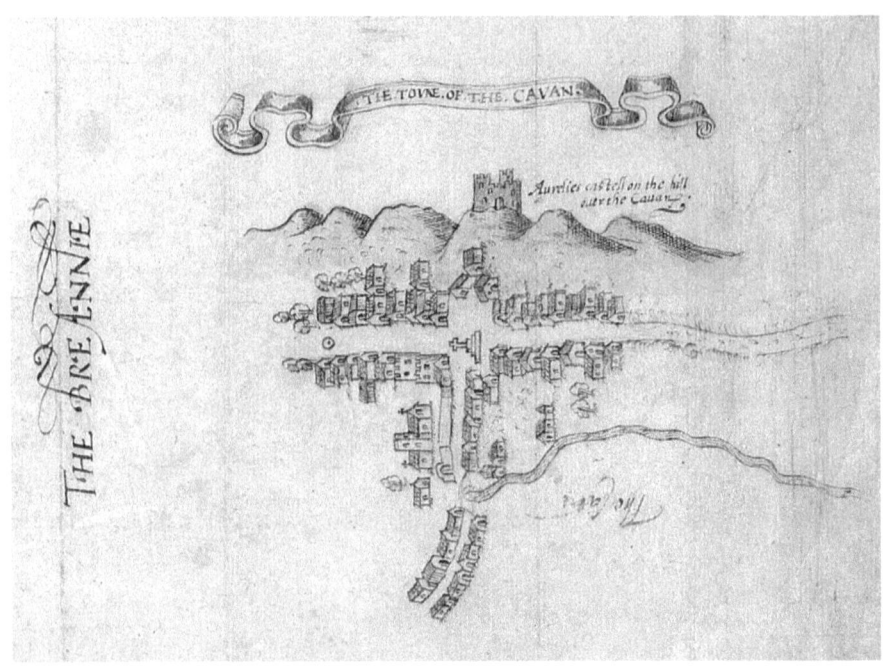

Figure 7: Map of Cavan town, *c.* 1590s: TNA, MPF 1/81. Courtesy of The National Archives

Figure 8: Clogh Oughter castle. Courtesy of Con Manning

them were sufficiently galled by our shot; that performed well, and observed their commands. For the first loose shot having discharged their parts retired, and with those unto whom they put themselves made good their ground, till by degrees retreating, they did altogether betake themselves to those places and duties appointed them for the defence of the castle. Some only charging of muskets, others discharging them from the flankers, windows, and battlements.

For now was the enemy approached; having first presented the defendants with a great piece upon carriages, planted on Windmill-hill, after our men had forsaken it, with which a battery was threatened, if they yielded not. But as it could not speak for itself, being but counterfeit, and made of wood; so did it work nothing upon them in the castle, who were wholly intent upon those who were now so near that they were under the command of their muskets.

The enemy finding many of their men to fall, retired under a rising of ground where we could not hurt them. Thence they sent and fired a stable, barn, other outhouses, and some stacks of corn, that they might march unseen under a cloud of smoke which the wind did to their great advantage drive upon the castle. Some of them with sheaves of oats, and straw burning, on the tops of their pikes ran to the flankers, thrusting them into those places whence the musketeers played upon them, by the fire and smoke to force them out; one of them adventurously laid hold of a musket in one of the spike-holes ready to be discharged. Thus came they on in a most desperate manner, being before made, to that end, more than half drunk with their aquavitae,[51] continuing in that headlong course about three quarters of an hour without gaining anything upon us (wanting scaling ladders) but losing themselves, their bodies being laid open to our shot from all parts, as the breaking up of the smoke gave way to discover them. Neither did their shot against our walls, windows, or battlements, of which they were not sparing out of such places of advantage whence we could not command them, do us any hurt. Thus having wearied themselves out in vain, and being at length sensible of their desperate undertakings, they now take care how to get off with least prejudice, they being no more to be gotten on by all that could be said or done by their commanders, I cannot say their leaders; for none of their officers would come up in all this service. Which being objected to them while they urged a second assault, one of the captains to show his forwardness above others would go on, and turning about to his soldiers he was met with a bullet which passed through

---

[51] Aqua vitae means 'water of life' and is another term for distilled alcohol, normally whiskey: Susan Flavin, *Consumption and culture in sixteenth-century Ireland: saffron, stockings and silk* (Woodbridge, 2014), pp 155–6.

both his checks, which was to him, and all his fellows, and followers a sufficient stop, from proceeding any further.

Whereupon they altogether retreated; now applying themselves to what they are more skilful in, the gathering together and taking away all the cattle that were without the castle, which they did, doing the like through all the way they went back, for six miles together, lest any should fall in the power of our men for their supply.

The shot in this fight was heard in the Castle Cloghouter two miles off by water, and the prisoners therein, seeing the fire and smoke, conceived Sir Francis his castle had been burnt.

In all this it could not be but very many of the enemy must have been killed, yet could we understand of no more than 167, few of those that were hurt ever recovering. One of ours was shot through a spikehole, another had his armour and doublet shot through, without further harm, who seeing the passage it had made, he told his fellow that it could not be but that he was a dead man, though he felt no hurt, neither could be persuaded till unbracing himself the bullet was found between his doublet and shirt. It is observed that in the whole service from the 23 of October til the 15 of June, setting aside such as were cut off in straggling, there were lost in fight, no more than five men belonging to this castle, one of them being Robert Mac Lalan a sergeant, who being taken at an advantage, was barbarously mangled having thirty-six wounds.[52]

Thus have we seen the end of this great undertaking, neither durst the enemy make another like approach for three months after; conceiving himself to have done sufficiently in placing guards upon bridges, and passes, many miles off, not thereby to make his way upon us, but to hinder our incursions (which he feared) upon his.

Yet could not this be any stop to Sir Francis Hammilton, who within two days after, breaking into the parts of the county of Leitrim to him adjoining, with twenty Horse and 100 Foot, having killed some stragglers (for others he met none) returned with forty cows and 200 sheep.

Desirous also to try the countenance of his neighbours placed by him (the enemy's guards about Bradies Bridge and the bridge of Ballihillian) and thence to bring in some corn for his supply, he sent out sixty musketeers with some women and youths, to carry away the corn being burnt out of the ear (as the fashion there is, when they want time to thrash), these being defended by the soldiers. The enemy being not far off appeared to the number of 200, yet durst they not deal with our men who had placed

---

[52] One 'Robert mc Lenan' was said in July 1642 to have been 'basely murthered' by Hugh McMaister and Turlogh mcCahill O Rely. It is unknown whether this is the same person or not: TCD, MS 833, fo. 170r.

themselves for their advantage, expecting the coming of Sir Francis who prepared for to second them, and after a while drew near with forty Foot, and forty Horse, whereof ten belonged to Sir James Craig. Upon approach of these the first who had before faced the rebels with a great shout break out upon them, and Sir Francis falling on, they fled, and being a little way pursued, ours retreated, esteeming it sufficient to have disengaged their fellows, and secured that small quantity of corn that was carried away. Our backs being turned, the enemy came on with a most terrible cry, as if we fled. Whereupon, Sir Francis making a stand, he mounted forty musketeers behind his horsemen and galloped after them, hoping to gain a place of strength which lay between them and the bridge, and so to engage them between his men. But they finding his intent, made from him thitherward, and having possessed themselves thereof, made themselves for resistance, of which we having killed one man, retired without being any further pursued, in the return, burning all before us.

About this time, the bloody sheriff thus disappointed of his cruelty, and for revenging on some what he suffered from others, commanded those poor British that were left in the town of Belturbet and not able to follow the rest, to be forced from off the bridge into the deep river, where they were all to the number of sixty swallowed up and perished.[53]

This being reported to those at Kylagh and Crohan, Sir Francis Hamilton, and Sir James Craig resolved on revenge, they going forth in several parties.

Sir Francis with 30 Horse and 100 Foot, drew to a place called Derewily bordering on the county of Leitrim, having intelligence of sixty rebels lying in a wood. To the place he came without discovery about the dawning of the day, surprising them in their cabins and beds; of whom twenty-seven he slew, taking fourteen prisoners, the soldiers being unwilling to reprieve any; these he after hanged, the rest escaping by reason of the wood. But fifty of Sir James Craig's Foot being by Sir Francis Hamilton appointed to attend any such occasion on the other side of the water (for a river was between them) they who escaped the one, fell into the hands of the other, of whom they slew ten and hanged four. Thus were all of the rebels used who after that time fell within their power.[54]

About the middle of March the store in both castles fell short, by feeding too many mouths: so that thenceforth they must fight for what they must eat; which they commonly did thrice a week, with very great hazard, for

---

[53] A death toll around the mid-thirties is more likely for this event: Scott, *Belturbet, County Cavan, 1610–1714*, pp 24–5.

[54] It seems that following the massacre in Belturbet, no quarter was given to Irish rebels. Dwindling supplies was likely another consideration.

there were placed 200 rebels to guard the passages in Sir James Craig's woods; 200 under Captain John O Reyly at Brady's Bridge, and Mulmore the great sheriff was now content himself to quarter in a cottage with 300 men about him at the bridge of Ballihillian, to keep our men from looking abroad.

On the 8 of April died Sir James Craig. A gentleman of singular and the best abilities; well deserving of his country both in peace and war: of whom I say the less because I cannot write enough.

The loss of this worthy person, as it could not but be of exceeding great disadvantage to the service: so did it double the pains, care, and charge of Sir Francis Hamilton, upon whom the oversight and ordering of matters in both castles was now cast. For at this time was the Lady Craig fallen sick & the company in the castle wasted by a mortal and infectious sickness, whereof there died 160, and the forces then remaining not sufficing for the guard of place. Whereby Sir Francis was enforced to send of his own for securing it: a squadron being daily from his castle of Kylagh, sent to Crohan, doing duty by turns, for no one would be persuaded to continue there, in respect of the infection, these were led out and brought off, by a strong guard to that purpose, sent twice each day placing the like number in Crohan, as they took out.

Necessity would not suffer them to be idle, therefore about the 22 of April, did Sir Francis Hamilton, with 210 foot and forty horse, taken out of both castles go forth to forage; and strong he must go, all places being strongly laid against him. He took his way towards Tullagha,[55] and under the covert of a wood laid an ambush of 150 men, sending the other, divided into two companies, together with women and boys, to gather in and drive away what cattle could thereabouts be met withal, commanding them if set upon by more than they could master, to make their retreat, and draw on the enemy, within the danger of the ambuscado which sorted accordingly for these foragers, were pursued by 300 of the enemy, who followed them until falling into the trap prepared for them: they being set upon fell into the wood, whither our Foot followed them, and as they fought their ways out from the Foot, the Horse that guarded the passages beat them back into the wood, in which hunting chase there were slain of them forty-five, of

---

[55] Tullyhaw is the most north-westerly barony in County Cavan. This barony, and its village, Ballymagovern, was the stronghold of the Gaelic McGovern family (here spelled 'Macgawran'). The aggressive actions in Cavan and Leitrim of many from that family, led by one Charles Magawran, are mentioned by British settlers in the depositions. Charles was one of the negotiators at the surrender of Keelagh and Croghan: TCD, MS 832, fos 167r; MS 833, fos 29r, 81r, 169r, 260r.

whom fourteen were of the sect of the Macgawrans, all landed men.⁵⁶ Few of the rest could have escaped, had not our men been called off by a discovery made by our scouts of another enemy approaching. Sir Francis having ordered his men for a second service, the rebels, though far exceeding in number, were content to suffer him to pass without any interruption bringing off with him sixty cows, which were divided between both castles.

In these and such daily and light services was the time taken up until the fourth day of May. For now the enemy finding that by their guards at distance they were but losers, as often as their loose companies encountered ours; and that therein they attained not their ends, which was the shutting us up from provision; being also informed that for want of victuals the castles could not hold out ten days; which was related to them by one Barlow, a fugitive, out of Sir Francis his castle where till then he & his had been relieved. They did therefore once more resolve to engage themselves upon it, and to make it their last work, concluding not to desist, or raise their siege till all were theirs.

To this end they drew up into Killishandra, and all the places about being at their first quartering about 2000, which was soon after made 3000, and that number doubled by the coming into the county of Cavan, of all those lords, gentlemen, and others who had been by our armies forced out of Meath, and other parts, besides the return of Philip Mac Hugh O Rely, with his men from Drogheda whence he was beaten off.⁵⁷

Thus were these two castles shut up at once without any intercourse. As for that of Crohan, besides their other wants, the besieged had their water without them,⁵⁸ which the rebels laboured to take away from them by shutting them up, as they should not without loss look out at the castle gates. To this purpose, they had in the night in a place of advantage cast up some works within less than half a musket shot from the gate, out of which by the valour of the defendants, they were more than once removed with loss, and their trenches cast down, yet did they as oft repossess themselves of them in the night and rebuilt with some further fortifications, what had been before demolished. By this means the distress for water was great within not having any but what by women or some others who in the night durst adventure forth, was brought in and sold to them at four pence the quart. But to make it wholly unserviceable, the rebels first cast into the well

---

⁵⁶ Jones means that these men had all received lands under the Plantation scheme.

⁵⁷ There was a siege of the town of Drogheda by the Irish in force from November 1641 until February 1642, when it was relieved by English forces: Lenihan, *Consolidating conquest*, pp 94–5.

⁵⁸ Jones means that the water supply was outside the castle walls.

a dead dog;[59] and after [that] the carcass of a man that had long been unburied. So that they were enforced to dig within the walls where they found water, but muddy and unwholesome.

In Sir Francis Hamilton's castle, provision of victuals was short, no bread was eaten there a fortnight before the surrender. Their milk cows reserved for giving milk to the sick were first killed; then most of their horses, after their dogs; and lastly they ate the hides of beasts slain many months before. The soldiers in these their sufferings began to mutiny, six or seven having run away with their arms to the enemy; the sickness of Sir Francis Hamilton occasioned by extraordinary pains, care, watching, and hard fare, adding to these discouragements.

These extremities thus suffered from the fourth of May, until the fourth of June; all supplies from Dublin being in vain expected more than seven months; there being also no hope left of any further subsistence where they were; Sir Francis now forcing himself out of his bed, began to entertain that treaty for quarter, which by the enemy had been daily offered, and till then was refused.

He desired in the first place that Master Thomas Price,[60] archdeacon of Kilmore, and Master Ambrose Bedell, chief in the castle of Crohan,[61] might be admitted with safety to confer with him that by their advice he

---

[59] Using dead bodies to pollute water supplies or to spread disease was a regular tactic of siege warfare.

[60] Thomas Price, a Welshman, was born *c.* 1599–1600 and took his B.A. and M.A. in Trinity College, Dublin, serving as vice-chancellor there in 1627, where he would have met William Bedell, who was appointed provost that year. Price was vicar of Drumlane (which neighbours Killeshandra) from 1634–61 and archdeacon of Kilmore from 1638–61. Having been trained by Bedell, to whom he was a 'a faithfull friend', it has been said that Price 'took great pains to instruct the native Irish through their own language'. See below for Jones' further comment on Price. He travelled to England, and was present at the Battle of Nantwich on 24 January 1644, as chaplain to the duke of Ormond's Royalist forces, at which he shot in the right eye. The eye, although darkened, was 'not destroyed'. Price later became bishop of Kildare and finally ascended to the archbishopric of Cashel: J.B. Leslie and D.W.T. Crooks, *Clergy of Kilmore, Elphin and Ardagh* (Belfast, 2008), pp 797–8; Shuckburgh (ed.), *Two biographies of William Bedell*, p. 114.

[61] Ambrose Bedell was the son of William Bedell, and he led the community at Croghan following the death of James Craig. Ambrose was imprisoned with his father, his brother (also William) and his brother-in-law Alexander Clogy on Clogh Oughter from December 1641 to January 1642. Ambrose gave a deposition on 26 November 1642, but did not discuss in it his time at Croghan: TCD, MS 83, fos 105r–6v.

might capitulate for both castles, which after much debate and some difficulty was condescended unto. From whom he having understood that the castle of Crohan was in no condition for longer resisting it was concluded that the treaty for surrender should precede.

On the one part appeared Philip Mac Hugh O Reley, the colonel, with Mulmore O Reyly the sheriff, and four other captains. On the other was Sir Francis Hamilton, Sir Arthur Forbes baronet (a gentleman about seventeen, yet one in all services), with two other gentlemen for the castle of Kylagh; and Master Price, and Master Bedall for Crohan. Between these certain articles were agreed upon as followed.

Article of agreement concluded and agreed upon, the quarter given by Philip Mac Hugh Mac Shan Rely, and the rest of the gentlemen here undernamed to Sir Francis Hamilton concerning the castles of Kylagh and Crohan, in manner and form following, bearing date the fourth day of June 1642.

1. In primis,[62] it is agreed by, and between these parties following, viz. Sir Francis Hamilton, knight and baronet, in the behalf of the Lady Mary Craige, himself, the gentlemen, gentlewomen, soldiers, and all others, both men, women and children, of what degree, condition, or quality whatsoever, belonging unto, or being in either of both castles viz. Kilagh and Crohan, shall have safe quarter from Philip mac Hugh Relie,[63] Edmond Relie,[64] Philip mac Mulmore Relie,[65] Mulmore mac Edmond Relie,[66] Hugh buii Relie,[67] John mac Philip Relie, Philip roe Relie,[68] James Neugent, R.A. Owen Rourke esquires,[69] Edmond mac Owen Relie,

---

[62] In primis is Latin for 'firstly'.
[63] See footnote 4 above.
[64] Edmund O'Reilly was the father of Mulmore.
[65] See footnote 24.
[66] Mulmore was, as we have seen, the sheriff of Cavan and one of the main ringleaders of the rising in the county.
[67] There were two Hugh Boy O'Reillys operating in Cavan at the time. One was from Kilduff in County Cavan, while the other held the rank of sergeant major in the Cavan company. Both were involved in a number of reported attacks on British deponents: TCD, MS 833, fos 197r, 204r.
[68] A Philip Roe O'Reilly had recently been in the Low Countries and was a captain in the Cavan Company: TCD, MS 833, fos 106r, 205v.
[69] An Owen Oge O'Rourke was named as attacking settlers in Cavan: TCD, MS 833, fo. 123r. It is unclear what the R.A. stands for.

Ferall oge Relie,[70] Charles mac Gauran,[71] Daniel mac Gauran,[72] John mac Kernan,[73] Conner Relie,[74] Relie, and Tirlagh, Cahil Relie, to be convoyed to Drogheda with safety of their lives, and of their bag and baggage,[75] which they shall carry with them and that such persons above named as are herein mentioned by particular name, viz. Philip mac Hugh Relie, Philip mac Mulmore Relie, Mulmore mac Edmond Relie, Philip roe Relie, Iohn mac Philip Relie, with such company as they shall think fit, shall go in person to guard us that are above mentioned, together with such a competent number of soldiers, a list being delivered unto Sir Francis Hamilton of their names as shall be sufficient to defend us from the danger or hurt of any that may assail us with any intention to hurt us, or any of us before mentioned, in our lives or goods. And it is likewise conditioned by the said Philip and the rest of the gentlemen above named, that they shall not leave us, until we be safely delivered over unto the hands of such a guard, or convoy, as shall be sent to receive us by the governor of Drogheda, and that we may be delivered over unto the hands of the said guard in love and amity, and depart so each from the other.

2. We shall have with us the king's majesty's arms, together with all carrabins, petronels, pistols, horsemen's pieces, bandoliers, swords, rapiers, daggers, horses, with all the horse furniture belonging to them, partisans, halberds[76] and that the soldiers belonging to Sir Francis Hamilton shall march away with drums beating, colours flying and bullets in their mouths.[77]

---

[70] A ffarrall oge Ó Rely was an insurgent from County Longford: TCD, MS 833, fo. 185r.
[71] Charles McGauran was from Tullyhaw barony and was involved in a number of attacks on British settlers: TCD, MS 833, fo. 128v.
[72] A Daniell mc Gawren was involved in the rising in Tullyhaw barony: TCD, MS 833, fo. 260r.
[73] An insurgent named John Kernan was named by a deponent: TCD, MS 833, fo. 169r.
[74] A Connor O Relly signed his name to a letter from Cavan in 1629 complaining about the Grace payments: Scott, 'Select Document: "Petition of the inhabitants of Cavan to the lord deputy and council"', p. 120.
[75] Similar promises had been broken at the outbreak of the rising in October 1641.
[76] A two-handed pole weapon, normally topped with a blade.
[77] In capitulation agreements, it was often stipulated that soldiers could hold bullets in their mouths in order to spit the ball or bullet into the musket barrel, which was probably already charged with gunpowder. The idea was that the soldier marching from the surrendered town or fortification could defend himself if the enemy attempted to break the agreement and attack the retreating soldiers. My thanks to Pádraig Lenihan and William Roulston for their discussions on this point.

3. Thirdly, we are to have provision provided for us, upon our way, which we are to march through for our ready moneys, the guard mentioned are to go upon their own charge.

4. Fourthly, we will be ready to depart by Wednesday the 15 of June 1642 and in the meantime, horses and carriage is to be provided for us for transporting of our baggage and sick people, if any shall happen to be at that time, either to be bought or hired for our ready money.

5. Fifthly that Master William Bedell[78] and his wife, Alexander Clogie,[79] Master Bagshaw and his family,[80] Robert Johnson,[81] together with all such British as are remaining within the county of Cavan, shall be sent hither to go along with the said Sir Francis Hamilton, and that they may have liberty to carry with them all such bag or baggage as they have to carry.[82]

6. Sixthly, that such poor men and women that are not able to go along with us, shall have a safe quarter to stay and remain in the country, and that provision shall be made for them, which unto Christianity appertains.[83]

7. Seventhly, that after both castles, viz. Kylagh and Crohan shall be surrendered, that then Philip mac Hugh Relie, and the rest of the gentlemen first named, shall take care that the said castles shall not be defaced, burnt, or demolished, but preserved for the king's majesty's use,

---

[78] William Bedell, eldest son of Bishop William Bedell, ended up in England, and recounts meeting his father's *bête noire*, Alan Cooke, in London in 1646: Shuckburgh (ed.), *Two biographies of William Bedell*, p. 124.

[79] Born in Scotland in 1614, Alexander Clogy was Bishop William Bedell's son-in-law. He held the vicarages of Denn and Urney in Kilmore and was part of Bedell's entourage which was imprisoned on Clogh Oughter in late 1641. He published in 1675 his biography of William Bedell, which forms part of Shuckburgh (ed.), *Two biographies of William Bedell*; Leslie & Crooks, *Clergy of Kilmore, Elphin & Ardagh*, p. 404.

[80] A Sir Edward Bagshaw was a planter with lands in the parish of Drumlane, which adjoins Killeshandra: TCD, MS 833, fos 33r, 282r.

[81] There was a Robert Johnston/Johnson who was James Craig's tenant in 1630: Hunter and Johnston, 'Men and arms', p. 7. A man with the same name gave a deposition in January 1642, so could not be the Robert Johnson referred to in this agreement: TCD, MS 833, fos 19r–v.

[82] Some settlers such as William Gibbs in Belturbet were not permitted to leave Cavan until 1643, even though they were capable of doing so: TCD, MS 833, fo. 249r.

[83] An interesting invocation of a shared religion here, given how both sides viewed each other's religious beliefs: Scott, *Belturbet, County Cavan, 1610–1714*, pp 22–3; Margey and Murphy, '"Backsliders from the Protestant religion": apostasy in the 1641 depositions'.

and for the use of the right owners thereof, and that the like care shall be had for preserving the gardens and orchards belonging to both castles.

8. Eighthly, that such people in both castles, that shall desire to travel to any part of this kingdom, shall be allowed so to do, and shall have passes given them for their safe travelling from one or other of authority within this county, and in the said passes it may be desired, that the gentlemen of such counties in which they are to pass through, may give them passes for their safe travelling unto such places as they shall desire to rest and remain in.

9. Ninthly, it is further agreed upon between both parties, that an authentic copy of this agreement sealed and signed by the said Philip mac Hugh Mac Shan Relie, and the rest of the gentlemen first named, shall be sent to Droghedah to the governor or chief commander there; to the end the said governor may send a certificate under his hand and seal, to be delivered unto Sir Francis Hamilton, and the rest of his company ten or twelve miles from Drogheda, for the security of both parties, and the due performance of this agreement, that there may be a certain place appointed by the said governor, where the said Sir Francis and his company shall be received without any danger or affront unto such as shall convoy them.

10. Lastly, for the due and true performance of this agreement, and every point therein contained, both parties shall make choice of the most principal gentlemen on either side to swear that they will truly and faithfully perform according to this agreement, and every point therein contained, and likewise set their hands and seals the day and year above written,

Philip Relie, Edmond Rely, Philip Rely, Mulmore O Rely, Hugh Rely, John Rely, Philip Rely, James Neugent, R.A. Owen Rourke, Edmond Rely, Ferall Rely, Charles mac Gauran, Daniel mac Gauran, Iohn mac Kernan, Conner Rely, Mulmore Relie, Turlagh Relie.

These articles being signed, sealed, and sworn unto by the subscribers, upon the 15 of June, there came out of the castle of Kylagh, Sir Francis Hamilton with about 800 men, women and children, of whom there were 230 fighting men. Out of Crohan with the Lady Craig there came about 400 of all sorts, and of them, 100 being serviceable men, and with these there were ten ministers, among whom Master Price, one of good abilities, diligent in his calling and forward in that service, doth merit especial respects. Besides those that came out of those castles, there were 140 others, who from other parts of the country joined themselves into them according as in the articles Sir Francis had provided for them.

These marched away according to the agreement with matches burning, bandoliers full and drums beating, and colours flying; bringing with them arms for ninety-five men. Sir Francis had in a trunk one firkin[84] of powder which was not discovered, leaving with the enemy only twenty pounds for to colour it. In both castles there were left about ninety pieces[85] great and small, and many pikes, most whereof had been recovered from the enemy.

These 1340 of all sorts were by Philip Mac Hugh Rely, with the rest of the mentioned in the articles for so doing, and a guard of 700 soldiers conducted towards Droghedah, they made a halt about fourteen miles from the town, expecting an answer from the governor, Sir Henry Titchburne, who about a mile from Slane, and eight miles from Droghedah, met them with two Troops, 300 Foot, the gross of both parts kept aloof, there being an hundred chosen out of each for to deliver and receive: all which was punctually observed on both sides.

From Droghedah, the said ten ministers, and above 1000 poor besides the poor soldiers, repaired to Dublin where now they are expecting conveniency of passage into England, if they may not be relieved there.

Sir Francis Hamilton, the lords justices, and council of Ireland, have recommended to the right honourable the lords commissioners for the Irish affairs, having for the present listed 100 of his own men under his command in the army. He deserving all encouragement and respects both for this prudence and forwardness in the public service, and his charity to the poor despoiled British, whom not only he relieved in his castle, but laid out great sums for clothing and feeding them in their going away.

This is the substance of all the chief passages of the rebellion in the county of Cavan, from the 23 of October 1641, until June 15, 1642, passing by Captain Culme's attempt for recovering the castle of Cloghouter,[86] with other passages, which with a more full discourse of what hath been formerly but briefly set forth, and the continuation there of, I refer to what I shall hereafter (God willing) set forth of the proceedings of the whole war in Ireland.[87]

---

[84] A firkin was a unit of measurement, normally one quarter of a barrel.
[85] Weapons, usually firearms.
[86] No accounts of Culme's attempt to retake Clogh Oughter seem to survive.
[87] Jones never published this account. He does not seem to have written it.

Appendix 1[88]

The acts of the synod of Kilkenny, May 1642

**In the name of the Holy Trinity, the Father, Son and the holy Ghost, Amen.**

Acts agreed upon, ordained, and concluded in the general congregation held at Kilkenny, the 10, 11 and 13 days of May, 1642 by those prelates whose names are subscribed. The proctors of such other prelates as then were absent, being present together with the superiors of the Regulars,[89] and many other dignitaries and learned men as well in divine, as also in the common law, with diverse Pastors and others of the Catholic clergy of all Ireland, whose names are likewise hereafter set down.

1. Whereas the war which now in Ireland, the Catholics do maintain against sectaries,[90] and chiefly against Puritans, for the defence of the Catholic religion for the maintenance of the prerogative and royal rights of our gracious King Charles for our gracious Queen so unworthily abused by the Puritans, for the honour, safety, and health of their royal issue, for to avert and refrain the injuries done unto them for the conservation of the just, and lawful safeguards, liberties and rights of Ireland and lastly for the defence of their own lives, fortunes, lands and possessions. Whereas I said this war is by the Catholics undertaken for the aforesaid causes against unlawful usurpers, oppressors and their enemies, chiefly Puritans. And that hereof we are informed as well by diverse and true remonstrances of diverse provinces, counties and noblemen, as also by the unanimous consent and agreement of almost the whole kingdom in this war and union. We therefore declare that war openly Catholic to be lawful and just, in which war, if some of the Catholics be found to proceed out of some particular and unjust title, covetousness, cruelty, revenge or hatred, or any such unlawful private intentions. We declare them therein grievously to sin, and therefore worthy to be punished and refrained with ecclesiastical censures (if advised thereof) they do not amend.

2. Whereas the adversaries do spread diverse rumours, do write diverse letters and under the king's name do print proclamations, which are not the

---

[88] This is also available online (entitled 'Articles agreed on by the Popish Synod, at Kilkenny, May 1642') at www.british-history.ac.uk/rushworth-papers/vol5/pp504-559.

[89] Monastic clergy who follow a Rule, such as the Franciscans and Augustinians.

[90] A sectary was a member of a religious body which was viewed as heretical. In this case, the Protestants are viewed by the Catholic synod as sectaries.

king's, by which means diverse plots and dangers may ensue unto our nation; we therefore to stop the way of untruth and forgeries of the political adversaries do will and command, that no such rumours, letters, or proclamations may have place, or belief, until it be known in a National Council, where they truly proceeded from the king, left to his own freedom, and until the agents of this kingdom hereafter to be appointed by a national council, have free passage to his majesty, whereby the kingdom may be certainly informed of his Majesty's intention and will.

3. Whereas no family, city, commonwealth, much less any kingdom may stand without union and concord, without which this kingdom for the present standeth in most danger. We think it therefore necessary that all Irish peers, magistrates, noblemen, cities and provinces, may be tied together with the holy bond of union and concord, and that they frame an oath of union and agreement which they shall devoutly and Christianly take, and faithfully observe. And for the conversation and exercise of this union, we have thought fit to ordain the ensuing points.

4. We straightly command all our inferiors, as well Churchmen as laymen to make no distinction at all between the old and ancient Irish, and no alienation, comparison or differences between provinces, cities, towns or families and lastly, not to begin, or forward any emulations, or comparisons whatsoever.

5. That in every province of Ireland there be a council made up, both of clergy and nobility, in which council shall be so many persons, at least as are counties in the province, and out of every city or notable town two persons.

6. Let one general council of the whole kingdom be made, both of the clergy, nobility, cities, and notable towns, in which council there shall be three out of every province, and out of every city one, or where cities are not, out of the chiefest towns. To this council the provincial councils shall have subordination, and from thence to it may be appealed, until this national council have opportunity to sit together. Again, if anything of great importance do occur, or be conceived in one province, which by a negative vote is rejected in the council of one province. Let it be sent to the councils of other provinces; except it be such a matter as cannot be delayed, and which doth not pertain to the weal public[91] of the other provinces.

7. Embassage[92] sent from one province to foreign nations shall be held as made from the rest of the provinces, and the fruit or benefit thereof shall be imparted, and divided between the provinces and cities which have more need thereof, chiefly such helps and fruits; as proceed from the bountiful liberalities of foreign princes, states, prelates or others whatsoever, provided always that the charges and damage be proportionally recompensed.

---

[91] The public good.
[92] This is the message or business carried by a messenger or ambassador.

8. If there be any province which may not conveniently send Embassage from itself unto foreign nations, let it signify it to another province, which may conveniently supply it, and ought in regard of their union to supply it according to the instructions sent from the other provinces concerning the place, and princes to which they would have their Embassages employed.

9. Let a faithful inventory be made in every province of the murders, burnings, and other cruelties, which are committed by the Puritan enemies, with a quotation of the place, day, cause, manner and persons, and other circumstances subscribed by one of public authority.

10. In every parish let a faithful and sworn messenger be appointed, whereby such cruelties, and other affairs may be written and sent to the neighbouring places, and likewise from one province to another. Let such things be written for the comfort, instruction and carefulness of the people.

11. Great men taken prisoners in one province, may not be set at liberty for any price, prayers, or exchange, without the consent of the prelates and nobility of the other province united, and let every province be careful of the liberties of such prisoners as are from the other provinces, as far as it conveniently may.

12. If anyone stubborn or dangerous be found in one province, county or town, let him be sent to another province, county or town where he may be safely kept, and (with less danger, or loss of others) remain.

13. Whosoever shall be declared in one county or province, adversary or traitor of this cause and country shall likewise be held, and punished in other counties and provinces, where he shall be found, and such as receive or favour him, or be his messengers knowing his misdemeanour, shall be liable to such punishment as the traitor himself.

14. We command and ordain as a main point pertaining to this union, that no province, county, city, town or person whatsoever shall demand peace, or submit himself to the enemies, without the consent of the general council of the whole kingdom and that under pain of excommunication to be incurred *ipso facto* and for further force of this statute to be observed. We will that in every province a firm oath be taken by the peers, nobility, corporations, and commonality of every province, and thereupon a public and authentical instrument be made. And that every province do send into every other province, an instrument subscribed, with the proper hands of such as have taken this oath, for the affordance of their oaths and who ever shall refuse to take this oath, let him be held as adversary of the common cause, and of the kingdom, and let him be punished, as such as hereafter shall be declared, except he be excused for the reasons hereafter to be set down.

15. The ordinaries of every place, the preachers, confessors, parish priests and other churchmen shall endeavour to see perfect peace and charity

observed between provinces, counties, cities, and families, as the obligation of this union required.

16. Such goods as well moveable as unmoveable pertaining to Catholics as were recovered from the enemies by this present war shall be restored to their former owners, provided that such necessary and reasonable charges shall be paid, as the next general or provincial council or committees of the county where the parties dwell, shall decree.

17. Whereas diverse persons do diversely carry themselves towards this cause, some with helps and supplies do assist the adversaries, others with victuals and arms, others with their advice and authority supporting as it were the contrary cause, some also as neuters behaving themselves, and others lastly neglecting their oath do forsake the Catholic union and cause. We do therefore declare and judge, all and every such as forsake this union, do fight for our enemies, accompany them in their war, defend or in any other way assist them as giving them weapons, victuals, council, or favour to be excommunicated and by these presents do excommunicate them. Provided that this present decree shall be first published in every diocese respectively and having received admonition beforehand, which shall supply the treble admonition otherwise requisite and we do hereby declare, so it be made in a place where it may easily come to the knowledge of those whom it toucheth. But as touching the judgement and punishment of the neuters we leave it to the ordinaries of every place respectively, so that the ordinaries themselves be not contrary to the judgement and opinion of this congregation, in which cause, we commit power to the metropolitans or archbishops to proceed against such ordinaries according to the common course of law wherein they are to be very careful and speedy, and if the metropolitans be found herein careless or guilty, let them be liable to such punishment as is ordained by the holy canons and let them be accused to the See Apostolic.

18. We ordain and decree that all and every such as from the beginning of this present war have invaded the possessions of the goods as well moveable as unmoveable, spiritual, or temporal of any Catholic, whether Irish or English, or also of any Irish Protestant being not adversary of this cause; and do detain any such goods, shall be excommunicated as by this present decree we do excommunicate them if admonished they do not amend and with the like censure we do bind such as henceforward shall invade or detain such goods, and not only them, but also all and every such as shall keep lands or possessions against public authority as also such as favour or assist them therein. And we declare involved in this censure, all and every of them who directly or indirectly hinder or forbid to pay their due rents unto such as have possessed the said lands from the beginning of this war and such likewise as without the licence of such possessors do take

or extort rents or equivalent payment from the tenants of such possessors under colour of paying soldiers therewith or otherwise.

19. We command all and every churchmen, as well secular as regular, not to hear the confessions of the aforesaid excommunicated persons, nor to administer unto them the holy sacraments under pain of excommunication *ipso facto*.

20. We will and declare all those that murder, dismember or grievously strike, all thieves, unlawful spoilers, robbers of any goods, extorters, together with all such as favour, receive, or any ways assist them, to be excommunicated, and so to remain, until they completely amend and satisfy no less than if they were, namely proclaimed, excommunicated, and for satisfaction of such crimes hitherto committed to be enjoined, we leave to the discretion of the ordinaries and confessors, how to absolve them.

21. Tradesmen for making weapons or powder brought into this country, or hereafter to be brought in, shall be free from all taxations and customers; as also all merchants, as shall transport into this country, such wares as are profitable for the Catholic cause, as arms and powder, may lawfully traffic without paying any custom, for commodities brought out of this kingdom, or transported hither of that kind and let this be proclaimed in all provinces, cities and towns.

22. We think it convenient, that in the next natural congregation, some be appointed out of the nobility and clergy as ambassadors to be sent in the behalf of the whole kingdom, unto the kings of France and Spain, to the emperor and his Holiness, and those to be of the church prelates, or one of the nobility and a lawyer.

23. We will and ordain, that ordinaries, dignitaries, and other proprietors of church livings, with the assistance of the colonel, or some other prime gentleman of the county, barony, or parish as the ordinaries, and dignitaries, or proprietors shall appoint, do set unto tenants, the lands, houses, tenements, and tithes, and other church livings, and let competent means be appointed for the maintenance of the said ordinaries, dignitaries and proprietors, and the rest to be appointed for the soldiers until it be otherwise ordained.

24. Collectors and receivers of the rents of church livings, shall be appointed by the ordinaries, with the consent of the proprietors in the presence of the chiefest gentlemen of every county, barony, or parish respectively.

25. The ordinaries and other proprietors of church livings may take unto themselves the houses, tenements and other church goods pertaining unto their respective titles, with obligations to pay proportionable rent unto the soldiers as aforesaid or his payment of their own competent maintenance

and let the houses, tenements and other church goods be taken from the Catholics, who heretofore had them as tenements or otherwise.

26. It is committed to the will and disposition of the ordinary whether and when to enter into the churches and celebrate Masses therein, we command all and every the general colonels, captains and other officers of our Catholic army to whom it appertaineth that they severally punish all transgressors of our aforesaid command touching murderers, maimers, strikers, thieves, robbers, and if they fail therein, we command the parish priests, curates or chaplains, respectively to declare them interdicted[93] and that they shall be excommunicated if they cause not due satisfaction to be made unto the commonwealth, and the party offended. And this the parish priests, or chaplains shall observe under pain of excommunication of sentence given *ipso facto*.

27. To the end that these acts, propositions and ordinances may have more happy success; we thought it fitting to have recourse unto God Almighty by prayers, fastings and alms. We therefore will pray and as far as it is needful do command that every priest as well secular, as regular do celebrate one Mass a week, and that all laymen do fast upon Wednesday, Friday, and Saturday in one week, and thence forward one day a week, and that upon Wednesday, or Saturday, as long as the ordinary shall please, and that they pray heartily unto God for the prosperous success of this our Catholic war, for which they shall gain so many days' indulgences, as every prelate shall publish in your several diocese[s] respectively after the fast of the aforesaid three days in one week, having first confessed, and received the blessed sacrament, and bestowed some alms to this effect.

28. In every regiment of soldiers let there be appointed at least two confessors, and one preacher, to be named by the ordinaries and by the superiors of the regulars, whose competent maintenance we commend and command to every colonel, in their respective regiments. And to the end that all those ordinances and statutes may effectually be put in execution, we will and decree that all archbishops, bishops, apostolical vicars and regular superiors, as well here present as absent, may be very serious and careful of the execution of the aforesaid, as they tender not to incur displeasure, wrath, and revenge, and herewith we charge their consciences.

29. Moreover, we pray and require, all noblemen, magistrates, and all other martial commanders, that with their helps and secular forces, they assist and set forward in execution, the aforesaid statutes in their several precincts respectively as often as it shall be needful. If in any of the aforesaid statutes any doubt or difficulty may by chance arise, the explication thereof we reserve to the Metropolitans in every province respectively, and to the

---

[93] A form of censure.

bishops in every their diocese, such of them as are no way contrary to this cause, no other person may presume to expound the aforesaid difficulties.

> Hac dicta, acta ordinata & statuta, subscripta erant nominibus sequentium Praelatorum.
>
> All those judgements, sayings, acts, and covenants, we submit to the judgement of the See Apostolic.
>
>> Hugo Archiepiscopus Armachanus.
>> Thomas Archiepiscopus Casselensis.
>> Malachius Archiepiscopus Guamenum.
>> David Episcopus Osoren.
>> Frater Boetius Episcopus Elphynensis.
>> Frater Patricius Episcopus Waterforden & Lismoren.
>> Frater Rochus Episcopas Kildaren.
>> Ioannes Electus Cluanfarten.
>> Emerus Electus Dunen & Conoren.
>> Frater Iosephus Everard, Procurator Archiepiscopi Dublinens.
>> Doctor Ioannes Creagh, Procurator Epsicopus Lymeriten.
>> David Bourck & Willielmus O Connell, Procurator Episcopi Imolacen.
>> Donatus O Tearnan, Procurator Episcopi Loanen.
>> Doctor Dionysius Harty, Decanus Laonensis.
>> Doctor Michael Hacket, vicar gener. Waterforden.
>> Gulielmus Devocer, vic. Gener. Fernesen.
>> Thomas Roch, Vicar Generalis Ossoren.
>> Frater Lucas Archer, Abbas Sancte Crucis.
>> Frater Anthonius de Rosario Ord. pred. vicar provincial.
>> Robertus Nugent, Societa Iesuin Heb.
>> Frater Thadeus Connoldus, Ang, pro provinc.
>> Joannes Wareinge, Decanus Lymericen.
>> Frater Patricius Darcye, Guardian Dublin.
>> Frater Thomas Strange, Guardian Waterford.
>> Frater Joseph Lancton, prior Kilkenniye.
>> Frater Tho. Tearnon, Guard. de Dundalk.
>> Frater Joannes Reyly, Guard Kilkennye.
>> Frater Boetius Eganus, Guard Buttevant.
>> Jordanus Boork, archidiaconus Lymericensis.

FINIS.

# Appendix 2
# Letter: Hugh Culme to Henry Jones, 4 August 1642

### The copy of a letter from Dublin, dated August 4, 1642

Loving brother,

Have been lately at Drogheda, about a lieutenant's place that was promised me; between that and Dublin, the rebels did fight with us; there were of ours, but seven of Captain Marow's troop, who were sent as a convoy for my Lord Blaney his son, some of their followers, and myself. The enemy was above fourscore Horse; we charged them four several times, and made them flee. We have two several armies gone out of Dublin, one towards Kells, being the way to the county of Cavan, the other to the county of Kildare. They have taken several castles, and left garrisons in them. The rebels dare not give our men battle, but we hear that they are very strong in Munster, and most of their forces of Meath, Monaghan, Tyrone, Fermanagh, and Armagh, are in the county of Cavan, where is their whole strength that can look upon these parts, and there are they strongly fortified. They have burnt all the towns and castles, not sparing their own dwellings, in the counties of Monaghan and Armagh. Here may appear how small their confidence is, while they burn their holds. The Scotch army is within three miles of Dundalk, and hath given the enemy many overthrows, so as they dare not meet them anymore. The Scots have taken from the Rebels about 6000 cows, and as many horses of all sorts. There were 2500 cows by the enemy, driven away from the Scots, which fell among the English army, so that what doth escape the one, the other doth take. They would be quickly subdued, if all things were right in England. Here is great want of money, whereby the soldiers are ready to mutiny. There is one Captain Vaughan commanding a troop of Horse, who is garrisoned in Dundalk; he with forty musketeers, and his Horse, did this last week go forth in the night to scout, and pillage abroad. Being about three miles from Dundalk, he met an Irish woman, whom he threatened to kill, if she told him not whence she came. She promised, so her life were spared, to do good service, and informed him that about seven miles thence, there was a very strong castle, wherein were 300 men well provided, and the place well stored with pillage, and that constantly, about one hour before day, the chiefest man among them went out to his devotions in a close adjoining to the castle, having the keys of the castle about him. The captain laid for him, and found it to be according to his intelligence; he suddenly laid hold on the man, whom having made sure, he opened the castle gate, and with his musketeers entered, where the rebels being surprised, they were all put to the sword, not one man of ours being lost. Here they found good store of good pillage. This is all the news I have for the present, &c

>Your loving brother
>Hugh Culme.[94]

---

[94] This is printed in pp 3–4 of Jones' *Relation*. Henry Jones was married to Hugh Culme's sister, hence the familiar greeting.

## Appendix 3[95]
## Remonstrance from County of Cavan to Lords Justices and Council at Dublin, 6th November 1641 and the response of the Council

**The humble remonstrance made by the gentry and commonality of the county of Cavan, of their grievances common with other parts of this kingdom of Ireland.**

To the right honourable the Lords Justices and Council.

Whereas we his majesty's loyal subjects of his highness' kingdom of Ireland have of long time groaned under many grievous pressures occasioned by the rigorous government of such placed over us, as respected more the advancement of their own private fortunes than the honour of his majesty, or the welfare of us his subjects, whereof we have in part in humble manner declared ourselves to his highness, by the agents sent from the parliament the representative body of this kingdom. Notwithstanding which we find ourselves of late threatened with far greater and more grievous vexations, either to the captivating of our consciences, our losing of our lawful liberties, or utter expulsion from our native seats, without any just grounds given on our parts to alter his majesty's goodness so long continued unto us; of all which we find great cause of fear in the proceedings of our neighbourly nations, and do see it already attempted upon us by certain petitioners, for the like course to be taken in this kingdom; for effecting whereof in a compulsory way, rumours hath caused fear of invasion from other parts, to the dissolving the bond of mutual agreement, which hitherto hath been held inviolate between the several subjects of this kingdom, and whereby all other his majesty's dominions have been til now linked in one.

For preventing therefore of such evils growing upon us in this kingdom, we have, for the preservation of his majesty's honour, and our own liberties, thought fit to take into our hands for his Highness' use and service, such forts and other places of strength as, coming into the possession of others, might prove disadvantageous, and tend to the utter undoing of this kingdom.

And we do hereby declare that herein we harbour not the least thought of disloyalty towards his Majesty, or purpose any hurt to any of his

---

[95] Taken from Gilbert (ed.), *Contemporary history of affairs in Ireland*, vol. I, part I, pp 365–7. See also *Cal. S.P. Ire., 1633–47*, pp 347–8.

Highness' subjects in their possessions, goods, or liberty; only we humbly desire that your lordships will be pleased to make remonstrance to his Majesty for us of all our grievances. We must have freedom of conscience and honest government. If any inconvenience has come, owing to the disturbances in the lower classes, to any people, English or other, we shall be ready, with the nobility and gentry, to cause restitution to be made. We beg for an answer at once. Signed,

    Philip Rely, Mulmore O'Reilly, Edmund Relly, Hugh Relly, Owen Relly, Hugh Reilly, Philip Relly, Ed. Reilly, Terlagh Relly.

## Answer from Lords Justices

First, that as in the beginning of this tumult the actors therein scandalised his majesty's sacred name and the State of England and Ireland as a colour to countenance their disorders, whereas we do declare in his majesty's name that they had no such power or authority from his majesty or any of his ministers, so now these petitioners have assumed a power to use the names of the gentry and commonality of the county of Cavan, whereas we well know that there are many of the gentry and commonality of the county of Cavan who gave the petitioners no such power, nor are any way consenting to the petitioners' proceedings. And the petitioners have also made mention in their said remonstrance of the other several counties of this kingdom, whereas it is well known to us that many other counties of the kingdom neither gave the petitioners any such power nor are any way consenting to their proceedings, and particularly all the English Pale have since this commotions begun petitioned this board, and like good and loyal subjects declared that they are none of that faction or confederacy, but are altogether averse and opposite to all their designs and all others of like condition as their ancestors have formerly been in all ages, which they are ready to manifest with the hazard of their estates and lives, which loyalty of theirs we do value as becomes us, and they will find comfortable fruits of it.

  Secondly, that the petitioners mention some fears they apprehend of great and grievous vexations, whereas there hath been no just cause given whence the petitioners should apprehend such doubts or fears, but those fears we conceive are now mentioned to colour such tumults and depredations as have been and are attempted.

  Thirdly, although the petitioners pretend that their taking into their hands certain forts and paces of strength was for his majesty's use and service, yet the petitioners and all men well know that by the laws and statutes of this kingdom no subject ought to take into his hands any forts or places of strength of his majesty's or any others in this kingdom without the express authority in that behalf of his majesty, so as the petitioners' acts are high presumptions unwarrantable and against all laws.

And albeit these proceedings of the petitioners and their adherents, aggravated with the robbing and spoiling of many of his majesty's good subjects, and their presuming to take up arms and to assemble forces without authority from his majesty, or us his justices, are acts of disloyalty in them against his sacred majesty, his crown and dignity, yet in compassion of the petitioners and for that we are informed that those who subscribed the said remonstrance have not had their hands in blood, and whom therefore we desire to reclaim, and to avoid the effusion of blood, which may follow by sending his majesty's forces against them and their adherents to reduce them to due obedience to his majesty and his royal authority. We are pleased hereby to declare that if the petitioners and their adherents in the county of Cavan will immediately peaceably return home to their own dwellings, as becomes dutiful and loyal subjects to do, and to their power procure restitution and satisfaction to be made to those whom they and their adherents have robbed of their lands, goods and chattels, and forbear to proceed hereafter in any acts of hostility or disturbance of the public peace or annoyance of his majesty's good subjects, which particulars we do hereby in his majesty's name and by his majesty's authority charge and command them to do accordingly, and thereof forthwith to give us advertisement, we will then transmit the said writing subscribed by them to his majesty, and humbly expect his royal pleasure therein.

Given at his majesty's castle of Dublin, the tenth of November, 1641.

>Lancelot Dublin Ormond, Ossory
>R. Dillon Cha: Lambert
>Ad: Loftus Jo: Temple
>Cha: Coote Rob: Merydith

>Ex: per Paul: Davys
>Endorsed: 10 Nov. 1641. Copy of the answer to the Remonstrance of the rebels in the county of Cavan.

# Bibliography

Adair, Charlene, 'The trial of Lord Maguire and "print culture"' in Eamon Darcy, Annaleigh Margey and Elaine Murphy (eds), *The 1641 depositions and the Irish rebellion* (London, 2012), pp 169–83, 235–8.

Bickley, F. (ed.), *Historical Manuscripts Commission: report on the manuscripts of the late Reginald Rawdon Hastings Esq. of the Manor House, Ashby de la Zouch* (London, 1947).

Boran, Elizabethanne (ed.), *The correspondence of James Ussher, 1600–1656*, 3 vols (Dublin, 2015).

Brady, Ciaran, 'The end of the O'Reilly lordship, 1584–1610' in David Edwards (ed.), *Regions and rulers in Ireland, 1100–1650: essays for Kenneth Nicholls* (Dublin, 2004), pp 174–200.

Caball, Marc, '"A star of the first magnitude": William Bedell (1571–1642), bishop of Kilmore and Gaelic culture' in Cherry and Scott (eds), *Cavan: history & society*, pp 173–98.

Cherry, Jonathan, 'The Maxwell family of Farnham, County Cavan: an introduction', *Breifne*, 42 (2006), pp 125–47.

Cherry, Jonathan, 'The indigenous and colonial urbanization of Cavan town, c. 1300–c. 1641' in Scott (ed.), *Culture and society in early modern Breifne/Cavan*, pp 85–105.

Cherry, Jonathan, 'The 1610 Cavan town charter: an introduction and transcription', *Breifne*, 45 (2009–10), pp 1–12.

Cherry, Jonathan, and Brendan Scott, 'Cavan town: an overview' in Scott (ed.), *Cavan town*, pp 1–18.

Cherry, Jonathan, and Brendan Scott (eds), *Cavan: history and society* (Dublin, 2014).

Clarke, Aidan, 'The commission for the despoiled subject, 1641–7' in Brian Mac Cuarta (ed.), *Reshaping Ireland, 1550–1700: colonization and its consequences* (Dublin, 2011), pp 241–60.

Clogy, Alexander, *Memoir of the life and episcopate of Dr William Bedell*, ed. W.W. Wilkins (London, 1862).

Cope, Joseph, 'Fashioning victims: Dr Henry Jones and the plight of Irish Protestants, 1642', *Historical Research*, 74:186 (2001), pp 370–91.

Cope, Joseph, 'The experience of survival during the 1641 Irish rebellion', *Historical Journal*, 46:2 (2003), pp 295–316.

Corish, Patrick J., 'The rising of 1641 and the confederacy, 1641–5' in T.W. Moody, F.X. Martin and F.J. Byrne (eds), *A new history of Ireland, III: early modern Ireland, 1534–1691* (Oxford, 1987), pp 289–314.

Culme, Arthur, *A diary and relation of passages in, and about Dublin* (London, 1647).

Cunningham, Bernadette, 'The anglicisation of East Breifne: the O'Reillys and the emergence of County Cavan' in Gillespie (ed.), *Cavan*, pp 51–72.

Davies, Oliver, 'The castles of County Cavan, part II', *Ulster Journal of Archaeology*, 3rd series, 11 (1948), pp 81–126 (reprinted in *Breifne*, 48 (2013), pp 43–89).

Davies, Oliver, 'The churches of County Cavan' in *R.S.A.I. Jn.*, 78 (1948), pp 73–118 (reprinted in *Breifne*, 48 (2013), pp 90–145).

Donovan, Brian C., and David Edwards, *British sources for Irish history, 1485–1641: a guide to manuscripts in local, regional and specialised repositories in England, Scotland and Wales* (Dublin, 1997).

Edwards, David, 'Out of the blue? Provincial unrest in Ireland before 1641' in Micheál Ó Siochrú and Jane Ohlmeyer (eds), *Ireland 1641: contexts and reactions* (Manchester, 2013), pp 95–114.

Flavin, Susan, *Consumption and culture in sixteenth-century Ireland: saffron, stockings and silk* (Woodbridge, 2014).

Ford, Alan, 'The reformation in Kilmore before 1641' in Gillespie (ed.), *Cavan*, pp 73–98.

Forkan, Kevin, 'Inventing an Irish Protestant icon: the strange death of Sir Charles Coote, 1642' in David Edwards, Pádraig Lenihan and Clodagh Tait (eds), *Age of atrocity: violence and political conflict in early modern Ireland* (Dublin, 2007), pp 204–18.

Forrestal, Alison, *Catholic synods in Ireland, 1600–1690* (Dublin, 1998).

Gilbert, J.T. (ed.), *A contemporary history of affairs in Ireland from 1641 to 1658* (Dublin, 1879).

Gillespie, Raymond (ed.), *Cavan: essays on the history of an Irish county* (Dublin, 1995, 2nd ed., 2004).

Gillespie, Raymond, *Seventeenth–century Ireland* (Dublin, 2006).

Gillespie, Raymond, 'Plantation Virginia revisited', *Breifne*, 49 (2014), pp 302–14.

Gillespie, Raymond and Brendan Scott (eds), *The Books of Knockninny: manuscripts, culture and society in early eighteenth-century Fermanagh* (Cavan, 2019).

Hamilton, George, *A history of the House of Hamilton* (Edinburgh, 1933).

Hayes-McCoy, G.A., 'Sir John Davies in Cavan in 1606 and 1610', *Breifne*, 3 (1960), pp 171–91.

Hill, George, *An historical account of the plantation in Ulster* (Belfast, 1877).

Hunter, Robert J., 'An Ulster Plantation town: Virginia', *Breifne*, 13 (1970), pp 43–51.
Hunter, Robert J., 'The English undertakers in the Plantation of Ulster [*recte* Cavan], 1610–41', *Breifne*, 16 (1973–5), pp 471–99.
Hunter, Robert J., *The Ulster plantation in the counties of Armagh and Cavan, 1608–1641* (Belfast, 2012).
Hunter, Robert J., and John Johnston (eds), *'Men and arms': the Ulster settlers, c. 1630* (Belfast, 2012).
*Inquisitionum in officio rotulorum cancellariae Hiberniae asservatarum repertorium*, ii (Dublin, 1829).
Jones, Henry, *A remonstrance of divers remarkeable passages concerning the church and kingdom of Ireland* (London, 1642).
Jones, Henry, *A relation of the beginnings and proceedings of the rebellion in the county of Cavan, within the province of Ulster in Ireland, from the 23 of October, 1641, untill the 15 of June, 1642* (London, 1642).
Jones, Henry, *A remonstrance of the beginnings and proceedings of the rebellion in the county of Cavan, within the province of Ulster in Ireland, from the 23 of October, 1641, untill the 15 of June, 1642* (London, 1642).
Kelly, Liam, *The diocese of Kilmore, c. 1100–1800* (Dublin, 2017).
Kelly, Liam, 'Prisons and punishments in County Cavan, 1600–1800', *Breifne*, 55 (2020), pp 597–605.
Lenihan, Pádraig, *Consolidating conquest: Ireland, 1603–1727* (Harlow, 2008).
Leslie, J.B., and D.W.T. Crooks, *Clergy of Kilmore, Elphin and Ardagh* (Belfast, 2008).
Little, Patrick, 'Michael Jones and the survival of the Church of Ireland, 1647–9', *Irish Historical Studies*, 163 (2019), pp 12–26.
Little, Patrick, 'The politics of preferment: the marquess of Ormond, Archbishop Ussher and the appointment of Irish bishops, 1643–47' in idem (ed.), *Ireland in crisis: war, politics and religion, 1641–50* (Manchester, 2020), pp 138–154.
Ludlow, Francis, and Arlene Crampsie, 'Environmental history of Ireland, 1550–1730' in Jane Ohlmeyer (ed.), *The Cambridge history of Ireland, volume II, 1550–1730* (Cambridge, 2018), pp 608–37.
Mac Cuarta, Brian, 'Ulster 1641: a select bibliography, 1993–2018' in Brian Mac Cuarta (ed.), *Ulster 1641: aspects of the rising* (3rd ed., Belfast, 2020), pp vi–xxii.
McCafferty, John, 'Venice in Cavan: the career of William Bedell, 1572–1642' in Scott (ed.), *Culture and society in early modern Breifne/Cavan*, pp 173–87.
McCaughey, Terence, *Dr Bedell and Mr King: the making of the Irish Bible* (Dublin, 2001).

McGrath, Bríd, 'A biographical dictionary of the membership of the Irish House of Commons, 1640–1641' (unpublished PhD thesis, Trinity College, Dublin, 1997).

McGrath, Bríd, 'Unconstitutional acts, violence, intimidation, vote-rigging, fraud and resistance: Cavan's parliamentary elections, 1613', *Breifne* (forthcoming, 2021).

Maginn, Christopher, 'Elizabethan Cavan: the institutions of Tudor government' in Scott (ed.), *Culture and society in early modern Breifne/Cavan*, pp 69–84.

Manning, Conleth, *Clogh Oughter Castle, County Cavan: archaeology, history and architecture* (Dublin, 2013).

Margey, Annaleigh, and Elaine Murphy, '"Backsliders from the Protestant religion": apostasy in the 1641 depositions', *Archivium Hibernicum*, 65 (2012), pp 82–188.

Moynes, Vera (ed.), *Irish Jesuit annual letters 1604–1674*, 2 vols (Dublin, 2019).

Nallen, Maura, 'A study of eight townlands in the parish of Killeshandra, 1608–1841', *Breifne*, 35 (1999), pp 5–84.

Ó Fearghail, Fearghus, 'The Catholic Church in County Kilkenny 1600–1800' in William Nolan and Kevin Whelan (eds), *Kilkenny: history and society* (Dublin, 1990), pp 197–249.

Ó Mórdha, Séamus P., 'Hugh O'Reilly (1581?–1653): a reforming primate', *Breifne*, 13 (1970), pp 1–42.

Ó Raghallaigh, Tomás, *Turbulence in Tullyhunco* (Cavan, 2010).

O'Reilly, Hugh, 'Lisnamaine Castle', *Breifne*, 23 (1985), pp 263–76.

Rooney, Dominic, *The life and times of Sir Frederick Hamilton, 1590–1647* (Dublin, 2013).

Roulston, William, 'The Scots in Plantation Cavan' in Scott (ed.), *Culture and society in early modern Breifne/Cavan*, pp 121–46.

Roulston, William, 'Landed society in Knockninny, c. 1660–c. 1740' in Gillespie and Scott (eds), *The Books of Knockninny*, pp 25–56.

Scott, Brendan, *Cavan 1609–53: plantation, war and religion* (Dublin, 2007).

Scott, Brendan (ed.), *Culture and society in early modern Breifne/Cavan* (Dublin, 2009).

Scott, Brendan, 'Accusations against Murtagh King, 1638', *Archivium Hibernicum*, 65 (2012), pp 76–81.

Scott, Brendan (ed.), *Cavan town, 1610–2010: a brief history* (Cavan, 2012).

Scott, Brendan, 'Accounts of the battle of Cavan town, 1690' in Scott (ed.), *Cavan town*, pp 19–27.

Scott, Brendan, 'The Ulster Plantation and its effect on native and settler in Cavan, 1610–41' in Cherry and Scott (eds), *Cavan: history and society*, pp 149–72.

Scott, Brendan, 'The strange burials and "afterlives" of William Bedell and James Craig' in Salvador Ryan (ed.), *Death and the Irish: a miscellany* (Dublin, 2016), pp 75–77.

Scott, Brendan, 'Select document: "Petition of the inhabitants of Cavan to the lord deputy and council", 8 July 1629', *Irish Historical Studies*, 43:163 (2019), pp 111–25.

Scott, Brendan, 'The Maguires and Fermanagh, 1603–1720' in Gillespie and Scott (eds), *The Books of Knockninny*, pp 11–24.

Scott, Brendan, 'Sir Stephen Butler and other inhabitants of early Plantation Belturbet', *Breifne*, 54 (2019), pp 416–26.

Scott, Brendan, *Belturbet, County Cavan, 1610–1714: the origins of an Ulster plantation town* (Dublin, 2020).

Shuckburgh, E.S. (ed.), *Two biographies of William Bedell, bishop of Kilmore* (Cambridge, 1902).

Treadwell, Victor (ed.), *The Irish commission of 1622: an investigation of the Irish administration 1615–22 and its consequences 1623–24* (Dublin, 2006).

# Index

Note: there has been some standardisation of place-names and surnames.

Aghalane, County Fermanagh, 48n
Aldrich, William, 24n
All Souls, Oxford, 2
Allen, Stephen, 9, 39n
Ardagh, deanery of, 2–3
Ardbraccan, County Meath, 24, 34, 38, 47
Athboy, County Meath, 34, 46

Bagshaw, Sir Edward, 61n
Bailey, Captain Robert, 37, 39, 47
Bailieborough, County Cavan, 6
Ballyhillian *see* Ballyheelan
Ballinagh, Cavan, 5, 39
Ballintemple, vicarage of, 3
Ballyconnell, County Cavan, 18
Ballyheelan, County Cavan, 48, 54, 56
Ballymagovern, County Cavan, 56n
Barlow, [–], 57
Barlow, Elizabeth, 15
Barlow, Randall, 15
Bedell, Ambrose, 17, 23, 58–9
Bedell, William, 3–5, 18n, 20, 21n, 23, 29, 30, 36n, 42, 49, 61n
Bedell Jr, William, 6, 10, 61
Belaneneagh *see* Ballinagh
Belturbet, County Cavan, 6, 8, 9, 10–12, 22, 24, 36–38, 40–42, 55, 61n
Bernard, Nicholas, 4
Black Bridge, County Cavan, 48
Blaney, Lord, 71
Book of Durrow, 29–30
Book of Kells, 29–30
Borlase, Sir John, 37
Brady, Owen, 41
Brady, Thomas, 18

Brady, Walter, 9, 18,
Brady's Bridge, County Cavan, 54, 56
Butler, Mary, 41
Butler, Stephen, 10, 41n

Carr, Raphe, 11
Castledine, Richard, 36n
Castlerahan barony, 6
Cavan, abbey of, 9
Cavan town, 6–9, 10–11, 19, 25, 36–8, 41, 47
Chichester, Arthur, 9, 17
Christ Church Cathedral, Dublin, 29
Clankee barony, 6
Clanmahon barony, 6–7
Clogh Oughter, 3, 18–22, 25, 36, 54, 58n, 61n, 63
Clogher, bishopric of, 28, 30
Clogy, Alexander, 14, 16, 21n, 23, 25, 58n, 61n
Clonmel, siege of, 21
Clonosey, County Cavan, 10
Cooke, Alan, 61n
Coote, Sir Charles, 13, 75
Craig, James, 12, 13, 14, 15–17, 20, 22–3, 24, 39–40, 47, 49, 55–6, 58n, 62
Craig, Lady Mary, 56, 59, 62
Creighton, David, 48
Creighton, George, 19
Croghan (Crohan), County Cavan, 13, 17, 24–5, 31, 39–40, 47, 49, 52, 55–9, 61–2
Cromwell, Oliver, 29, 30
Cromwell, Richard, 29
Culme, Amedas, 21
Culme, Anna, 21

81

Culme, Anthony, 20–21
Culme, Arthur, 19–22, 25, 36, 63
Culme Jr, Arthur, 21
Culme, Benjamin, 17, 22
Culme, Elizabeth, 21
Culme, Hugh, 9, 17–21
Culme Jr, Hugh, 25, 31, 71–2
Culme, Jane, 17, 28
Culme, Mary, 21
Culme, Philip, 21

Dalys Bridge (Mountnugent), County Cavan, 38
Dickson, Timothy, 11
Dollymoch, Wales, 2
Doobally, County Cavan, 13
Dowdall, [–], 43
Drogheda, County Louth, 25, 34, 37, 44–8, 50–51, 57, 60, 62–3, 71
Drumgoon, parish of, 24n
Drumlane, parish of, 58n, 61n

East Breifne, 5
Edinburgh, 16
Emerson, Godfrey, 1, 30
Emmanuel College, Cambridge, 3
Erne River, 10–11
Essex, England, 3

Farnham, County Cavan, 22, 23n, 36
Fermanagh, County, 3, 7, 9, 34, 37, 43, 45, 71
Fingall, earl of, 19
Fitz-Simonds, [–], 52
Forbes, Sir Arthur, 13
Forbes, Jr, Sir Arthur, 13n, 59

Hamilton, Sir Alexander, 13
Hamilton, Claud, 12
Hamilton, duke of, 14,

Hamilton, Sir Francis, 11, 12, 13–15, 16, 21n, 22–5, 31, 37, 39, 40, 47–50, 52, 55–63
Hamilton, Jane, 13
Hamilton, Malcolm, 48
Hill, Moses, 16

Inishconnell, County Cavan, 20

Jamestown, County Leitrim, 13
Johnson, Robert, 61
Jones, Lewis, 2–3
Jones, Michael, 29
Jones, Theophilus, 18n, 29

Keelagh (Kylagh), County Cavan, 13–14, 17, 24–5, 31, 37, 47, 52, 55–6, 59, 61–2
Kells, County Meath, 25, 29, 30, 34, 45, 46, 71
Kildrumferton, vicarage of, 3
Kilkenny, Synod of (1642), 25, 31, 64–70
Killaloe, bishopric of, 2
Killeshandra, vicarage of, 3
Killeshandra, County Cavan, 6, 8, 12–13, 17, 24, 37n, 39n, 49, 52, 57
Kilmore Cathedral, 3, 5
Kilmore, deanery of, 3–5
Kilmore, vicarage of, 3
Kilmore and Ardagh, bishoprics/dioceses of, 3–4, 19–20
Kylagh *see* Keelagh

Leitrim, County, 2, 3, 13, 16, 49, 51, 54, 55, 56n
Lismore, Cavan, 23, 40n, 43n
Loughtee barony, 6, 7, 8, 10, 19

# INDEX

Magawran *see* McGovern
Maguire, Conor, 7, 37
Maguire, Rory, 37, 38
Marow, Captain, 71
Maxwell, Robert, 36n
Mayot, Thomas, 3
McGovern (McGauran), Charles, 56, 60, 62
McGovern (McGauran), Daniel, 60, 62
McKernan, John, 60
Mac Lalan, Robert, 54
McLenan, Robert, 54
McMaster, Hugh, 54n
McSweeney, Eugene, 3–4
Meath, County, 3, 24, 34, 57
Meath, bishopric/diocese of, 2, 29, 30, 38
Moore, Archibald, 18
Moore, Charles, 38

Navan, County Meath, 34, 46
Neugent, James, 59
Nugent, Robert, 51

O'More, Rory, 7
O'Neill, Eoghan Roe, 18n, 45n
O'Neill, Phelim, 7–8
O'Reilly, Conner, 60, 62
O'Reilly, Edmund, 48, 50, 59–60, 62, 74
O'Reilly, Edmund MacOwen, 59
O'Reilly, Ferall, 62
O'Reilly, Hugh, 35n
O'Reilly, Hugh (archbishop), 25
O'Reilly, Hugh Boy, 59
O'Reilly, John MacPhilip, 59–60
O'Reilly, Captain John, 56
O'Reilly, Sir John, 9
O'Reilly, Mulmore (Myles), 11, 22, 23–4, 35, 40n, 44, 50–51, 56, 59–60, 62, 74
O'Reilly, Owen, 36, 74

O'Reilly, Owen Mac Turlagh, 21
O'Reilly, Patrick, 9
O'Reilly, Philip MacHugh, 11, 22, 31, 35–6, 38, 42, 50–51, 57, 59–63, 74
O'Reilly, Philip Mulmore, 11, 21, 23, 40, 43, 59–60, 62 74
O'Reilly, Philip Roe, 59–60
O'Reilly, Turlagh, 62, 74
O'Reilly, Turlough MacCahill, 54
O'Rely/O'Reyly, etc *see* O'Reilly
O'Rourke, Brian, 59
O'Rourke, Fr, 50
O'Rourke, Laughlin, 49
O'Rourke, Owen, 50, 59

Parsons, William, 37
Philpott, Edward, 41
Piers, Mary, 28
Piers, Sir William, 28
Plunkett, Oliver, 29
Price, Thomas, 58–9, 62

Relie/Rely, etc *see* O'Reilly
Ridgeway, John, 19
Rothe, Bishop David, 25
Ryves, Captain Richard, 11, 24, 37–8, 46–7

St Andrew's Church, Dublin, 29
St Patrick's Cathedral, Dublin, 17, 19
Sexton, George, 18
Sheridan, Denis, 4
Somerville, James, 48
Stanihurst, Margaret, 2

Talbot, Walter, 18
Templeogue, County Dublin, 46
Titchburne, Henry, 63
Togher, County Cavan, 5
Trim, County Meath, 34, 46

Trinity College, Dublin, 2, 3, 29, 30, 58n
Tullygarvey barony, 6–7, 18
Tullyhaw barony, 6–7, 18, 56n, 60n
Tullyhunco barony, 6–7, 12–13, 15,
Tullymongan Hill, Cavan, 8–9
Tullyvin, County Cavan, 18

Ussher, Arland, 2
Ussher, James, 2, 4, 29
Ussher, Mabel, 2

Vaughan, Captain, 71
Venice, 3
Virginia, County Cavan, 6, 10, 16, 19, 43, 46

Waldron, John, 23n, 36n
Waldron, Sir Thomas, 36n
Westmeath, County, 28, 51
Windmill-Hill, County Cavan, 52, 53
Wotton, Sir Henry, 3

www.ingramcontent.com/pod-product-compliance
Lightning Source LLC
Chambersburg PA
CBHW030042100526
44590CB00011B/304